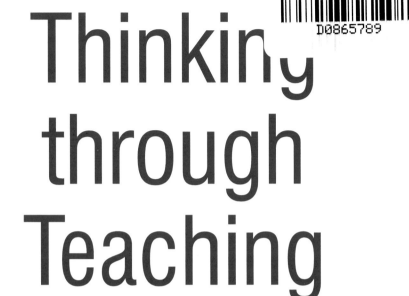

Thinking through Teaching

A framework for enhancing participation and learning

SUSAN HART

with contributions from
Niv Culora, Lesley Higgs,
Una Pattrick and Penny Travers

David Fulton Publishers
York St. John College

About the author

Susan Hart worked for sixteen years in secondary and primary schools, training initially as a teacher of French and English. After further training in language and literacy development, she taught English and integrated humanities and, in her role as learning support teacher, worked collaboratively with teachers in many different subject areas to explore ways of enhancing pupils' participation and learning. She later moved to the primary sector, again working collaboratively with class teachers to support literacy and learning in the primary phase. She currently works with experienced teachers engaged in courses of continuing professional development and in collaborative research.

David Fulton Publishers Ltd
Ormond House, 26–27 Boswell Street, London WC1N 3JD. www.fultonbooks.co.uk

First published in Great Britain by David Fulton Publishers 2000

Note: The right of Susan Hart to be identified as the author of this work has been asserted by her in accordance with the Copyright, Designs and Patents Act 1988.

Copyright © Susan Hart 2000

British Library Cataloguing in Publication Data
A catalogue record for this book is available from the British Library

ISBN 1–85346–628–X

Typeset by Kate Williams, Abergavenny
Printed in Great Britain by The Cromwell Press Ltd, Trowbridge, Wilts.

Contents

Acknowledgements

This book owes a great debt to many teachers, pupils and colleagues, and especially to:

- the commitment, enthusiasm and insight of the group of teachers who took part in the research organised by the Enfield Language and Curriculum Access Service (LcaS): Niv Culora, Deb Harris, Lesley Higgs, Gita Lakhlani, Karen Kennedy, Ülfet Mahmout, Emer O'Dowd, Neil Parr, Una Pattrick and Penny Travers;
- the individual pupils who provided the focus for their research (whose names have been changed to protect anonymity, and whose permission has been sought, as far as possible, to reproduce material of a directly personal nature);
- other teachers who contributed their experiences to the book, and especially Ros Frost, Nicky Hancock and Sue Taylor;
- Mary Jane Drummond, for her unrivalled capacity to enable me to see things differently which has played an important part in the development of the ideas in this book, and for much valued feedback on early drafts of the manuscript;
- Alison Foyle, at David Fulton Publishers, for her encouragement and editorial support;
- Christine Goad, who provided invaluable secretarial support;
- the following publishers who have given permission for previously published material to be reproduced here: Sage Publications, for the use of extracts from Chapter 4 of Molnar, A. and Lindquist, B., *Changing Problem Behaviour in Schools*; Multilingual Matters, for the use of Fig. 1.3 from Cline, T. and Frederikson, N., *Curriculum Related Assessment, Cummins and Bilingual Pupils*; Cassell, for the use of extracts from Claxton, G., *Teaching to Learn*; Blackwell, for the use of Fig. 17 from Hull, R., *The Language Gap*;
- the Language and Curriculum Access Service in the London Borough of Enfield (now LcaS Developments) for permission to use extracts from *Enabling Progress in Multilingual Classrooms: Towards Inclusive Education* and *Making Progress: Teaching and Assessment in Multilingual Classrooms*;
- Ian Mitchell for permission to use illustrations drawn from *Enabling Progress*.

Introduction

Thinking through teaching is a vital part of teachers' professional work. It is that critical phase in the teaching cycle when teachers review and reflect on previous experience in such a way as to draw out the lessons to guide future work. It is an aspect of teaching that easily gets crowded out by the many other pressures on teachers' time, yet it is crucial to make space for it because it affords one of the most important sources of teachers' power to make a difference to children's learning.

This book offers a practical approach to the task of thinking through teaching which can support teachers in using whatever time they do have as constructively and productively as possible. The approach encourages teachers to focus particularly on those aspects of their work that surprise, puzzle or concern them. For instance, why did the activity that went so well with one group of children fail to engage another? What lay behind those seemingly 'wrong' or irrelevant answers to questions? What can be done to make learning more meaningful for those who are struggling or who seem to find little to capture their interest and imagination at school? The approach involves bringing existing knowledge and expertise to bear on teachers' own questions and concerns in such a way as to generate new insights and understandings that can guide the development of practice. I call this approach 'innovative thinking'.

Innovative thinking is a process of reflective analysis designed to assist in *moving beyond* existing perceptions and understandings. The process makes use of five distinct questioning 'moves' that help to probe the meaning of classroom events from a number of different angles. As I shall explain in more detail in Chapter 2, these questioning moves are not meant to be followed rigidly or in any particular order. Their function is to help keep in mind the many different perspectives from which we can seek to understand children's learning. They support the creative process through which new insights and understandings are generated, and provide the basis upon which we can have confidence in using new ideas emerging to inform future teaching.

The book is intended for both experienced and newly qualified teachers, and for those undergoing initial teacher training. The need to reflect on and learn from experience does not diminish in importance the more expert and experienced teachers become. It is a capacity which all teachers need to develop from the earliest stages of their training, and which continues to be a central and essential feature of professional practice throughout their professional lives. The book is designed to help any teacher to use and strengthen their powers of creative and critical thinking in the interests of children, with a view to enhancing participation and learning.

In an earlier book (Hart 1996) I describe the research that led to the development of the ideas presented here. I explain how the notion of 'innovative thinking' emerged from my study of two children's writing development, specifically as a means of addressing concerns about children's learning in mainstream educational settings. I describe how the various questioning 'moves' came to be identified, and the basis for my conviction that these simply name and describe interpretive processes that many teachers will recognise themselves using in the course of their everyday teaching. Since this earlier book was published, I have had the opportunity to see how teachers working in a variety of mainstream settings have used the ideas to support the development of their work. I have been able to discover, through their experience and feedback, if the questioning 'moves' do indeed name and describe processes that they themselves are familiar with and aware of using in the course of normal teaching; and if the approach itself was actually of use in supporting their retrospective thinking about their work.

In particular, the approach has been tried out and developed by a group of teachers in the London Borough of Enfield (Language and Curriculum Access Service 1999). Mainstream teachers in primary and secondary schools who were working collaboratively with Section XI* partnership teachers used 'innovative thinking' to help them explore how to enhance the participation and learning of bilingual children whose progress was giving cause for concern. Each pair of teachers chose one or two children to focus on. Over the course of a year, they undertook to give additional thought to these children's engagement with classroom learning experiences and to generate ideas for adapting and developing existing provision. They tried out these ideas, monitored their impact on the child's learning, reflected on what to do next, and so on. Each teacher kept a journal in which she recorded her ongoing thinking and the developments in practice that resulted from it. Other evidence, in the form of observations of children, conversations with them, samples of work, was also collected and preserved in order to have a record of developments over the year.

Many of the practical examples used in this book are drawn from the insights and ideas developed by this group of teachers (in some cases drawing directly on transcripts of group discussions, as well as documentary evidence and written accounts). Chapters 8 and 9 offer detailed accounts of their thinking about individual children and how this informed the overall development of their work with the whole class. They wish to emphasise that, although their concerns were focused on bilingual children, this is not in any sense to imply that bilingual children's learning often or usually gives their teachers cause for concern. This focus came about as a result of the particular purposes for which they chose to try out innovative thinking, which are explained in more detail in Chapter 11.

Looking back over the year, the teachers confirmed that they had indeed found the various questioning 'moves' to be familiar, and were able to recognise themselves using them in the course of their everyday thinking. They did not find it so easy, though, at

---

* Now Ethnic Minority Achievement Grant

first, to make conscious and deliberate use of the moves to structure and guide their analysis of classroom experience. However, as familiarity with the moves increased and as evidence gradually accumulated regarding important insights that had been opened up as a result of the use of different perspectives, so teachers' belief in the value and utility of the approach strengthened. Now they say that when reflecting upon a concern, or making an interpretation, they automatically question their thinking from different points of view. More conscious and systematic use of the questioning moves that support the process of innovative thinking has come to be an integral feature of their professional work.

Moreover, they found themselves using and adapting the approach not just for the purposes of teaching and learning in the classroom but as a support for professional thinking generally. Some teachers described how it had helped them to think through problematic situations arising with colleagues as well as with children. Others have used it as an analytic tool when carrying out classroom research as a basis for developing ideas for more general improvement of their practice. I also understand that nurses and social workers studying on post-qualifying courses of professional development have been able to adapt the framework for their own use; that they have found it a valuable tool for exploring and generating ideas to guide the development of their professional work (Winter and Munn-Giddings forthcoming).

I hope, therefore, that this book will be of interest and relevance to a wide range of practitioners working in the caring professions. Although the approach has been specifically developed and adapted to fit the professional context of classroom teaching, experience suggests that it can easily – and with only minor changes of emphasis and terminology – be transferred to other professional situations where practitioners seek to learn from experience in order to inform future decision-making and guide the development of their work.

Overview of the book

The book is organised into four main parts. Part One sets out to explain and justify the overall approach to review and reflection proposed in the book. The first chapter sets out the values that underpin the approach presented here, using vignettes drawn from teachers' experience. Chapter 2 introduces the framework of questioning moves that supports the process of thinking through teaching, and explores the links between these questioning moves and the existing strategies that teachers use to make sense of what happens in their classrooms.

Part Two looks at each of the five questioning moves in detail, drawing on teachers' experience, research and literature. The five chapters illustrate the range of ideas and resources upon which we might call when viewing classroom events from a particular perspective. They also illustrate how the ideas of others can be used to extend, enrich and challenge existing thinking.

Part Three provides detailed examples of developments in teachers' thinking and practice that came about as a result of using the framework for innovative thinking to assist them in reviewing and reflecting on their own work. Chapter 8 continues the story of a pupil, Asad, begun in Chapter 1. It offers a detailed study of two primary teachers' work with a Year 4 boy who did not seem to be deriving much understanding from the learning experiences provided. Chapter 9 offers a detailed account of two secondary teachers' work with a Year 7 Turkish-speaking girl, Ayse, who did not seem to be involved in class activities. Both chapters document the strategies that teachers devised in the light of their developing understanding, and show how these helped not only to foster the individuals' participation and inclusion, but also to enhance learning opportunities for the whole group.

Part Four considers the wider relevance and applicability of the ideas presented in the current context. Acknowledging the demands and counter-pressures that make it difficult for teachers to give priority to thinking and developmental work of the kind described, it may be possible nevertheless to translate external demands, requirements and national policy directions into policies that do encourage and support an innovative approach to professional work. Chapter 10 looks at school development issues, and explores the scope for extending teachers' opportunities for working together to review and reflect on their teaching in the context of a development agenda that is, in large part, externally driven. Chapter 11 looks at the relationship between innovative thinking and schools' responsibilities for providing support for children experiencing difficulties, examining these issues particularly from the perspective of bilingual children whose progress is giving cause for concern. Chapter 12 concludes the book by exploring the relationship between the view of teaching, and learning through teaching, presented here and other current accounts of the nature of teachers' thinking.

PART ONE

CHAPTER 1

In fairness to children[*]
Why thinking through teaching is so vital

Why is it so vital that teachers do take time to revisit and reflect on classroom experience? In this chapter, I explain the basis for the main theme of the book: that the process of thinking through teaching is one of the most important sources – if not *the* most important source – of teachers' power to make a difference to children's learning. I use examples drawn from real-life classrooms to illustrate that we cannot fulfil our essential responsibilities and commitments as teachers without an active commitment to the retrospective analysis of teaching.

The trouble with Costas

The first example is concerned with the consequences of judgements arrived at in the course of our moment-by-moment interactions with children. It illustrates how important it is, in fairness to children, that we take time to review and reflect on judgements made about individual children and their learning, especially when these reflect negatively upon children's qualities and capabilities.

This incident took place in a Year 1 classroom, shortly before lunch time, when everyone was clearing up. The teacher involved, Emer, asked for a volunteer to take a game down the corridor to the library and put it on the table there. Unusually, six-year-old Costas was the first to raise his hand. Pleased at this initiative, Emer gave him the box. He chose a partner to go with him, and off the two boys went.

Five minutes later, realising that they had not returned, she went to the classroom door to look for them. To her surprise, there they were outside the door, still holding the box. Suppressing an impatient sigh (and thinking 'why does Costas *never* listen to instructions?'), she asked what they were supposed to be doing with the game. No reply. She rephrased her question. Costas shifted about uneasily and started explaining how to play the game. He seemed to be totally confused. Emer explained again, slowly and carefully, what she wanted them to do, and this time, thankfully, the errand was successfully accomplished.

---

* For the title of this chapter I owe a debt to Morwenna Griffiths and Carol Davies (1995), whose book bears the same title, although the notion of 'fairness' is used somewhat differently here.

Emer's first reaction was to log this interaction in her mind as further confirmation of her concerns about Costas, who, she felt, 'never listens to instructions' and 'is in a world of his own a lot of the time'. As she walked down the corridor, though, after the lesson, and began to review the incident in her mind, a number of different interpretations started occurring to her. For instance, knowing that the Incey Wincey Spider game was Costas's favourite, she wondered if perhaps, having seen the game and heard the start of her sentence 'I want someone to . . .', Costas had jumped to the conclusion that the teacher was inviting volunteers to play the game, not to put it away. It may not have been that he didn't *listen* to her instructions, but that, in his excitement and desire to be chosen, he heard what he *thought* she was going to say. Indeed, since there was a lot of noise and bustle going on because of the clearing up, he may not have been able to *hear* clearly her exact words.

Emer realised that because *she* knew that it was lunch time, she had assumed that the children *also* knew, and therefore it did not occur to her that they might interpret her request as an invitation to play a game. But was this a reasonable assumption? Had it been explicitly stated? Young children often find it difficult to judge the passage of time, and clearing up is not necessarily a reliable guide. The library was a place where small groups of children often went with a teacher to play a game. And why would Emer have invited Costas to choose a partner to go with him, if the task was simply to put the game away rather than to play?

If this was Costas's interpretation, it might explain why, five minutes later, he was outside the door with the box under his arm (waiting for Emer to join them?), and why he said what he did when Emer questioned him about what he was supposed to have done with the box. If he appeared 'confused' when answering Emer's questions, this may have been an understandable response to a situation where he was getting the message that he had somehow failed the teacher, yet not knowing what it was that he had done. He was still trying to make sense of what was wanted of him from within his own frame of reference, but becoming more hesitant as he lost trust in his own understandings.

As Emer explored these alternative ways of interpreting what had happened, she found her initial, rather negative, judgements being transformed into an encouraging perception of Costas acting competently within his own frames of reference. It took Emer only a few moments to do the thinking described here. Yet doing so fulfilled a vital responsibility towards Costas, enabling her to question rather than reinforce a negative view of his learning. This changed perception, in turn, helped to bring about a subtle shift in the dynamics of her relationship with him.

This was, in one sense, a trivial interaction, but for Costas the consequences were far from trivial. If Emer had left her immediate interpretation unquestioned, it would have provided one more bit of evidence reinforcing her view of him as someone who 'does not listen to instructions' and is 'in a world of his own'. These perceptions would have continued to influence Costas's classroom experience and shape his identity as a learner within the class group. Fortunately for Costas, she took time to check out her judgement and consider other ways of interpreting what happened. In the process, a new understanding of the situation emerged, helping to free herself and Costas from what might otherwise have become a self-perpetuating cycle.

The conditions of classroom life are such that teachers are always under pressure. One of the skills that teachers develop is an ability to make rapid judgements about what is going on and what action is required, and to move smoothly to action much of the time without consciously deliberating alternatives. Yet, as this incident shows, reliance on intuitive judgement may not, in some cases, always serve children's best interests. Once Emer had carried out this analysis, she realised how her pre-existing view of Costas had influenced her interpretation on this occasion. The interpretation that first sprang to mind fitted with what she expected to see and screened out many other features of the situation which needed to be taken into account in order to arrive at a fair judgement, and have confidence in using this to inform teaching.

As soon as Emer had a bit of space to think, she was able to generate a much more complex, contextualised understanding of what had occurred, which shed a quite different light on Costas's response. Her considered analysis explored possible connections between Costas's apparent failure to carry out the instructions and features of the *context* in which the request was made. She tried to remember what she had actually said, in order to see if there might have been some ambiguity or unnoticed complexity about the way in which she had phrased her instructions. She recalled the inevitable noise and bustle in the classroom at clearing-up time which might have affected the audibility of what she had said.

Her considered analysis also managed to pinpoint some *assumptions* about shared knowledge – the fact that it was lunch time – which may not in fact have been shared by Costas, and so contributed to the breakdown in communication. She brought to mind relevant knowledge of the child – his love of that particular game – which helped to appreciate how he might have been prompted to construe the situation differently from her. This in turn triggered a realisation of how the invitation to choose a partner could easily – and perhaps more logically – have been interpreted as fitting Costas's meaning rather than her own. In achieving this insight, she needed to move outside her own existing frame of reference and try to see the situation afresh from the *child's point of view.*

She also took account of the way that her spontaneous *feelings* of impatience may have affected both what occurred and the sense she made of it (she was tired, it was the end of the morning, she was suffering from a heavy cold). Although she took steps to check whether or not Costas knew what she had asked him to do, before making the judgement that 'he had not listened', she was aware of suppressing a sigh of impatience on finding the two boys outside the classroom door, and this may well have communicated itself to them. She realised that their lack of response might not be an indication that they did not know what they were supposed to be doing, but that they were reading her displeasure and trying to work out how to respond to *that*. They were responding not to her question but to its subtext, reflected in her body language. Moreover, the negative feelings may unconsciously have caused her to give emphasis to the more negative, rather than the more positive, readings of the situation, that she was readily able to bring to mind in her reflections outside the classroom.

Emer's thoughtful reconstruction of these particular classroom events reminds us how cautious we need to be in the authority that we give to *any* interpretations of children's learning, and especially those which construct the meaning of the situation in terms of deficiencies of the child's characteristics or abilities. Our interpretations are constructed through a process of meaning-making which is highly complex and uncertain. The understandings that we reach depend upon the possibilities that we consider (whether consciously or intuitively), which in turn depend upon the limited time, information and resources available. As Emer's analysis shows, the high speed at which interpretations and judgements have to be made in a busy classroom mean that the significance of what is occurring may be missed. It is therefore always possible that retrospectively we will discover a new meaning which shows children's activities in a quite different light. Every act of making meaning simultaneously excludes alternative possibilities, and those alternatives may be lost from view permanently if we do not have time to go back and review our earlier thinking in the light of subsequent experience, or if it does not occur to us to question existing interpretations.

This is one important reason why, in fairness to children, it is so vital for teachers (to the extent that time and circumstances allow) to revisit their classroom experience – their judgements as well as their actions – and explore the implications for future work. All day long, in the context of fleeting encounters of this kind, teachers make judgements about the meaning of children's responses that contribute to an accumulating picture about each child. We pay little attention to them, yet they help to shape our expectations and these expectations in turn guide our subsequent interactions with the child and the learning opportunities that are made available. Though we may never explicitly give voice to them, they are subtly communicated to children and help to shape the way that children perceive themselves as learners, and how they behave in response to our teaching.

The example of Emer and Costas shows that taking time – however brief – for detailed, systematic reflection on classroom experience can transform perspectives in ways that profoundly affect the course of children's school experience. Moreover, teachers need not fear that the time invested in such retrospective reflection benefits only those individuals. After discussing this experience with colleagues, Emer resolved to stop and think every time she found herself making negative judgements about children's responses in the course of ordinary teaching. Although the conditions of classroom life do not allow much opportunity for extended deliberation, she increasingly found that, when a child did something ostensibly 'wrong', she was able to suspend judgement for an instant and look at the response afresh from the child's perspective. Gradually, this became quite a 'routine' response which she was able to incorporate flexibly into her teaching.

The benefit of hindsight

Classroom dynamics are so complex and children's responses so unpredictable that it is impossible for teachers to foresee, in every case, how their well-intentioned words (instructions, suggestions, questions, requests and invitations) might be open to misinterpretation or simply construed in ways which they did not expect or intend. It is often only once the child has done something unexpected – and maybe undesired – that we are able to recognise and make explicit the tacit assumptions and expectations informing our thinking, and consider any possible mismatch between these and the interpretations arrived at by the child.

Another of the teachers in the Enfield research group (see Introduction p. v) reported an occasion when she was surprised to be presented by a Year 4 child with a story carefully written out in capital letters. She was surprised because her current assessment of the child's development in this area was that he did have a reasonable understanding of the appropriate use of capital letters. She was about to revise this assessment and consider what action to take, when she suddenly remembered an inter-action with the child, shortly before he had begun writing, which she had concluded by saying to him 'Remember your capital letters!'

It occurred to her that the child might have written the piece in capitals because he thought that this was what the teacher was urging him to do. Maybe what he understood was 'Remember to write in capital letters'. He then went on obediently to follow this instruction, even though it conflicted with what he knew and understood to be the appropriate use of capital letters in the context of ordinary writing. Teachers' purposes are frequently not entirely transparent to children – maybe the piece written in capitals was less an indication of limited understanding of punctuation than an indication of the child's willingness to defer to the teacher's assumed purposes, even when these did not make very good sense to the child.

It was only once the child had responded by writing the piece in capitals that the teacher was in possession of the evidence that alerted her to the possible ambiguity associated with her original instruction. It was only then that she was in a position to reconsider what had occurred in the light of her knowledge of the child, and reshape her understanding accordingly. In this case, the memory of what she had said and its possible impact on the child's response was recalled to mind, there and then on the spot, as she registered her surprise and reflected upon how to react. The realisation that she might have unwittingly misled the child influenced both the way that she responded to him at the time and her judgement about what follow-up might be needed.

Learning from experience

As well as revising spontaneous judgements, the retrospective analysis of teaching also provides the means for continually refining, adjusting and developing practice in the light of children's responses. Through this means, we take steps to ensure that whatever can be done *is* done to enhance children's participation and learning. This is particularly important when children do not appear to have learnt what we hope and intend that they will learn, as the following example illustrates.

Two teachers, Niv and Una (the co-authors of Chapter 8), were working with their Year 4 class on a history topic on the Tudors. Although they often struggled to find time to plan activities jointly, on this occasion they had managed to plan very carefully. The purpose of the afternoon's activities was to encourage the children to explore why the Spanish Armada had failed. There was a lively story/presentation on video, followed by carefully structured tasks using plenty of visual support material. Children were actively encour-aged to work collaboratively and talk ideas through together. Niv and Una felt that they had planned the activities in a way that would support the learning of every child, including and especially Asad – a boy of Bangladeshi heritage – whose learning was giving them some cause for concern. However, Asad did not respond as they had hoped to the activities. He took a long time to settle down and seemed distracted a lot of the time. He did not make use of the support provided (e.g. teacher modelling, working in pairs, opportunities for discussion); and an exchange with him at the end of the afternoon suggested that he had not grasped the main points of the lesson.

Niv and Una were disappointed that the activities had not been more successful in promoting Asad's learning, and that he had not made more use of the support strategies available. They had assumed and expected that the children would have the opportunity to talk the ideas through orally as well as in writing; yet Asad had chosen to work alone. It was possible, of course, that Asad's response that afternoon was affected by something quite unconnected with the task or learning context; but since he was responding to a situation that they were directly instrumental in creating, they saw it as their responsibility to think back carefully over what had occurred in order to see if there was anything that they could have done differently that would have been more helpful for Asad, and consider how they might use this insight to inform future planning.

Classroom dynamics are so complex that it is impossible to predict or fully control what will happen when decisions made at the point of planning are translated into practice. As Mary Jane Drummond has convincingly argued, 'unless planning is tied to a rigorous process of review, it remains in the domain of wishful thinking' (Drummond 1993: 154). It is as much a part of teachers' professional responsibilities to *review* classroom happenings and try to learn from experience, as it is to *plan* thoroughly, organise carefully and strive to *interact* thoughtfully and sensitively with children in the classroom.

Taking time to review our beliefs and practices in the light of experience is especially important when the evidence suggests that some children have not derived much benefit from the learning activities. Niv and Una saw Asad's response to this lesson as feedback to themselves about their endeavours to create a learning environment that would be supportive of every child. It was the lesson that they were disappointed with, not Asad; and they were very concerned that he should not interpret any 'failure' in understanding as his own.

However, the feedback provided by children's responses does not yield up readymade answers. We have to process it carefully in order to discover what it may have to tell us about the scope available to us for refining and adjusting features of the learning environment in order to foster more successful learning. Why, for instance, did Asad decline the opportunity to work collaboratively? Was it anything to do with the task, or how the invitation to collaborate was presented? Could anything else have been done – before or during the lesson – that might have made a difference to Asad's disinclination to work with others? Was there perhaps something else going on with Asad that afternoon that made him want to be on his own?

Questions such as these begin to open up the situation to fresh examination and suggest possible areas where adaptations might usefully be made. In Chapter 8, Niv and Una describe in detail how the questions that they found themselves asking, in processing the feedback provided by Asad's response to their lesson, helped to bring about significant developments in thinking and practice. The ability to ask the kinds of questions that foster new understanding and the development of teaching is an essential part of teachers' professional expertise. Every teaching session yields a rich resource for teachers' thinking and learning, but that potential will remain untapped unless we analyse, reflect upon it and use it to gain a deeper understanding.

That is why the process of review has such an important part to play in the overall teaching-learning cycle. To the extent that Asad's teachers were able to exploit that potential, Asad would be able to look forward to continual refinements and adjustments to the learning environment made with his needs and interests in mind. Without the process of review, any barriers that were currently limiting Asad's successful engagement with the school curriculum, or leading his teachers to perceive this engagement as problematic, would remain unexamined.

A priority focus for thinking through teaching

Some sort of review is, of course, happening spontaneously as we go about our work in the classroom. During activities, we are continuously monitoring events in light of our expectations and intentions and making adjustments accordingly. As several children ask for help relating to the wording on a task sheet, we register the existence of a problem or ambiguity of language and make a mental note to look at this again and perhaps revise it. We observe how effectively – or otherwise – particular groupings of children are cooperating on particular tasks, and perhaps make mental notes to change key group members or provide opportunities for developing listening skills.

Nevertheless, so much happens during the course of a teaching session that it is impossible to pay careful, critical attention to everything. We take in far more information than we can ever process thoroughly so we have to prioritise where we focus our attention for the purposes of review. In this book, I propose that we focus particularly upon those aspects of children's learning about which we register some significant questions or concerns during the course of our day-to-day teaching: an individual or group of children in class who do not seem to be gaining what we hope and expect from our teaching; some aspect of children's response which we found puzzling, or which was not what we anticipated or desired.

Although the approach can equally well be used to learn from any situation – including those in which learning activities have been unexpectedly successful in engaging children's interest and fostering learning – it is especially important, in fairness to children, to give time to careful review of those aspects of our experience which fall short of our hopes and aspirations, in order to see what might be learnt from them. As many of the examples presented in this book will show, an analysis focused on an individual or group does not necessarily benefit only those individuals – it can generate new understandings that influence teachers' work generally, and open up possibilities for practice that can enrich and enhance learning opportunities for the whole class.

In this chapter, I have argued that the process of thinking through teaching is a vital part of the everyday work of all teachers – not something to be undertaken occasionally or just by teachers whose work is judged (by themselves or others) to be in need of improvement. When teachers' existing knowledge and expertise are combined with the fresh evidence of children's engagement with learning activities, we have a powerful resource for gaining new insights and understandings to guide the development of practice. The better able we are to use our existing resources to learn from experience, the more we can do to improve and enhance the quality of learning for all children.

CHAPTER 2

Worrying about Asad
A framework for innovative thinking

What does the process of thinking through teaching entail? How can we use whatever time we do have for this vital aspect of our work as constructively and productively as possible? In this chapter, I introduce a particular approach to the task of thinking through teaching that I hope teachers will find useful in supporting and strengthening their own ways of reviewing and reflecting on their work. I call this 'innovative thinking' because it involves asking ourselves the kinds of questions that help to generate new ideas and understandings to guide the development of practice.

The approach makes use of five questioning 'moves' (see Figure 2.1). Their function is to help keep in mind the many different perspectives and angles from which we can seek to understand the meaning of a situation, or child's learning, each of which has its own unique insights to offer. Many teachers will no doubt recognise these moves as reflective strategies which they do in fact already use spontaneously as part of the process of making sense of what is going on in their classrooms and intervening to support and promote learning. All that is new about this approach is that it makes more conscious and deliberate use of these strategies, and uses them *together* to extend and challenge existing thinking.

Using them prompts teachers to draw on the vast reservoir of relevant knowledge about the dynamics of learning and teaching which they have acquired through experience, training and reading, and to use this knowledge creatively in seeking to gain new insight into some aspect of their practice that they have identified as requiring further thought. It is through the achievement of new understanding that we become able to see new possibilities for enhancing children's participation and learning in practice (Hart 1996).

In order to introduce, in a concrete way, the questioning moves that support the process of innovative thinking, I shall take up again the story of Asad begun in the previous chapter. With his teachers' consent, and without pre-empting their own account of their work with Asad (in Chapter 8), I will show how the five questioning moves *could* be used to support and structure the process of review. I will examine the kinds of questions that might be asked and further possibilities that might be opened up through the use of each of the moves, and explain how the five moves can be at their most powerful when used flexibly together to question and extend existing thinking.

The five moves that make up the framework for innovative thinking

Making connections	This move involves exploring how the specific characteristics of the child's response might be connected to features of the immediate and wider learning environment.
Contradicting	This move involves questioning the assumptions underlying a given interpretation by searching out a plausible alternative interpretation which casts the meaning of the situation in a contrasting light. This helps to tease out the norms and expectations underlying the original interpretation so that this can be re-examined.
Taking a child's eye view	This move involves trying to enter the child's frame of reference and to see the meaning and logic of the child's response from the child's perspective.
Noting the impact of feelings	This move involves examining the part that our own feelings play in the meaning that we bestow on the situation and in leading us to a particular interpretation.
Postponing judgement in order to find out more	This move involves recognising that we may lack information or expertise needed to have confidence in our judgements. It involves holding back from further analysis and the attempt to arrive at judgements about the child's needs while we take steps to acquire further information.

Figure 2.1   A framework for innovative thinking

A framework for innovative thinking: introducing the five questioning moves

The starting point for innovative thinking is the particular reading or interpretation of classroom events which leads the teacher to feel puzzled, concerned or keen to give further thought to some particular aspect of the situation. In Asad's case, the starting point is the perception that *he has not understood the main points of the lesson.* This is not an objective statement of fact, of course, but an interpretation arising from what Asad was observed doing and saying during the course of the lesson.

To recall, Asad's teachers had taken great care in planning a lesson associated with their history topic, trying to build in as many supports for understanding as possible in the hope that Asad and the other children would learn about cause and consequence in relation to the defeat of the Spanish Armada, as well as successfully using a variety of sources to extract information. But they were disappointed to discover, in conversation with Asad at the end of the afternoon (see Figure 2.2), that he did not seem to have grasped the main points of the lesson.

In carrying out the analysis, this interpretation is used as a springboard for asking questions of different kinds. The five questioning moves outlined below are used flexibly, and in interaction with one another, not in a step-by-step way or in any particular order. They are introduced separately for the purposes of clarity in explaining what is distinctive about each.

Teacher:	Asad, why do you think the Spanish didn't win?
Asad:	That man, you know . . . the boss, he was told to drive the ship or King Philip would chop his head off.
Teacher:	The boss? Oh you mean the Duke of Sidonia?
Asad:	Yeh . . . but you see he was being sick and couldn't see where he was going so he drived the wrong way.
Teacher:	Then what happened?
Asad:	The British, yeh, they sended sticks, big sticks . . . logs to the Spanish and fired their ships and all the . . . um, um . . . those long things for bombing, they exploded.

Figure 2.2   Did Asad understand the main points of the lesson?

Making connections

This first move encourages us to explore how Asad's perceived *failure to grasp the main points of the lesson* might have been connected to features of the immediate and wider learning environment. In the previous chapter, for instance, we looked at the possibility that the quality of his understanding might have been affected by his decision not to work with a partner, and that this decision in turn might be linked in various ways to features of the immediate learning context that were susceptible to influence by the teacher.

Connections might also be explored between Asad's perceived difficulties in understanding and other features of classroom language and communication. What kinds of language demands were made by the various tasks? Might these have presented unexpected barriers to understanding? How accessible was the language used in the video and printed resources the children were required to use? Were there confusions or complications due to unfamiliar vocabulary or layout? How did pictures and headings assist children in drawing out the 'main ideas'?

It would be relevant, too, to think about teacher–pupil interaction and how the task was actually introduced to the class. What steps were taken to negotiate the overall purpose with the children and how clear/concrete was the initial presentation? How attentively did the class – and particularly Asad – listen? How long did the scene setting last? Where was Asad seated while the teacher was talking? Did his positioning within the group affect his ability to sustain interest and attention? What opportunity did the children have to clarify their purposes in watching the video before viewing? Did they know in advance how they would be drawing on the video for subsequent work?

Questions such as these help to contextualise Asad's perceived difficulties and focus attention on features of the learning environment that might be susceptible to modification. Experienced teachers know that all these factors (and many more) can affect the quality and extent of children's engagement with classroom tasks. If we can gain new insight into the dynamics that are helping to produce a particular kind of response, this may suggest ways of intervening to adjust or change features of the situation in order to encourage more successful learning.

Of course, there are limits to the changes and adjustments that individual teachers are in a position to make. Asad's teachers might, for instance, question the content of the activity because of its remoteness from the children's experiences, purposes and relevances; but with a statutory curriculum, their freedom of manoeuvre with respect to the content of what is taught is inevitably limited. Nevertheless, there are many different strategies that teachers can use to help children to make personally worthwhile connections between what they know and are interested in and the content laid down in the programmes of study.

The ability to ask contextualising questions about a child's perceived difficulties relies on teachers' understanding of the many features of school and classroom life that influence children's learning. It demands a sophisticated appreciation of the complexities of classroom dynamics, and an understanding of how the interacting worlds of school, home and community also impact on children's responses in the classroom. Used on its own, however, this move leaves many significant features of the situation unexamined. Not least, it leaves unquestioned the original interpretation that Asad had failed to grasp the main ideas of the lesson. Just as important as contextualising an interpretation is scrutinising the interpretation itself.

Contradicting

This second move is based on the conviction that the interpretation that immediately springs to mind is not necessarily the *only* interpretation that could be made. It involves looking afresh at the evidence and searching out plausible alternative readings of the situation which *also* fit with the evidence. An alternative interpretation may cast what was previously seen as a 'problem' in a different light, and suggest different ways of responding. The process can also operate in reverse, when an initially positive interpretation is countered with one or more less positive readings.

In Asad's case, for example, knowing that English is his second language (he speaks Bengali at home) might cause us to question whether the problem (if there is one) might be not so much one of lack of understanding but of difficulty in *expressing* his understanding in English. Perhaps Asad knew and understood far more than he could put into words effectively. Perhaps he chose to make reference to those features of the lesson which he could readily express in language, and left out those aspects that were more linguistically complex to communicate. This would have a considerably distorting effect on his *account* of the 'main points', disguising what might in fact have been a far more adequate overall understanding.

This 'contradicting' move plays a very important part in the process of innovative thinking because it challenges the expectations and assumptions implicit in our judgements. If we judge something to be a problem, there is always an implicit norm being invoked against which the situation – or child's response – is being measured and judged deficient. In Asad's case, there was an expectation regarding appropriate kinds of statements that children *ought* to be able to make to sum up the main points of the lesson. Once we have made this expectation explicit, we are in a position to reconsider whether or not it is reasonable, or whether we might make some adjustment to our expectations such that Asad's response would cease to be seen as a cause for concern.

Thinking about Asad raises interesting questions about learning and the legitimacy of learning outcomes that are not part of the intended curriculum. On reflection we might come to see Asad's response as indicating not so much *lack* of understanding as a *different* understanding of the lesson from the outcome planned for and anticipated by his teachers. Are we are able to recognise and value outcomes that are different from those that we anticipated yet which arise from the active engagement of the child's own thinking? And if it is important to ensure that learning proceeds on common ground, how do we ensure that the teacher's perception of the key points communicates itself to learners in a way that fosters genuine understanding, rather than a transitory ability to offer the 'right' answers when questioned?

The two moves, *making connections* and *contradicting*, complement one another because each looks at an aspect of the situation that the other leaves unexamined.

- 'Making connections' accepts the teacher's original interpretation of events, but recognises the child's response as an outcome of complex processes that are susceptible to reshaping by the teacher. Searching out connections between Asad's perceived lack of understanding and features of the learning environment opens up possibilities for adjusting classroom learning experiences in order to enhance Asad's participation and learning.
- 'Contradicting' focuses on the interpretation itself and questions the basis for judging the child's response a matter for concern. It involves scrutinising the assumptions underlying the judgement in order to reassess if these are fair and reasonable, and exploring plausible alternative ways of construing the child's response that would cast it in a different, more positive light.

Asad's teachers would want to be sure, in fairness to Asad, that the perception of his lack of understanding had been examined from *both* points of view. On the one hand, we would want to be sure that whatever steps could be taken *were* taken to foster Asad's understanding. On the other hand, our efforts would be fruitless – and might even compound the problem – if we were to pursue them without questioning our *own* taken-for-granted understanding of the main points of the lesson; if we were to impose this understanding on the child rather than considering the legitimacy of the child's own meanings and trying to communicate with the child on the basis of those meanings.

From within our own frames of reference, we can recognise the possibility that what initially was perceived as lack of understanding or misunderstanding might in fact reflect a *different* rather than a *deficient* understanding on the part of the child. In order to explore more fully that alternative understanding, however, we need to be able to take an imaginative leap outside of our own accustomed ways of seeing the world, and try to see the situation afresh through the child's eyes.

Taking a child's eye view

This third move requires us to set aside our teacher, and adult, frames of reference and try to understand the meaning and logic of the child's behaviour as it might make sense to someone whose knowledge and experience are very different from our own. In Asad's case, we might look again at the conversation that initially prompted concern on the part of Asad's teachers and ask ourselves what this can tell us about what Asad actually has taken from the lesson. Why has he chosen to focus on these particular elements? What is their appeal from his point of view? What do they tell us about what has captured Asad's interest, about the knowledge and assumptions that he brought to the task, or about the sense that the activities actually made to him?

We might try to think ourselves into Asad's position as a learner during the course of the lesson and imagine how he felt about the task that he was carrying out. What did he think that he was doing in this lesson and why? Was his sense of purpose to do with understanding or merely task completion? It is important, too, to recognise that the learning task that was central to his teachers' purposes may not have been all that central to Asad's experience in the course of that afternoon. Children have their own agendas which do not necessarily coincide with those of their teachers. The cognitive content of classroom tasks could be a secondary issue for a child who was preoccupied with personal problems external to the classroom, or with difficulties arising in his social relationships with classmates. If such difficulties were Asad's preoccupation, the 'main point' of the session, in his terms, might well have been simply to manage the situation in such a way as to escape taunts or other forms of unwelcome attention from other children. Hence, possibly, his choice to work alone.

Trying to move out of our own frames of reference and view the situation through the child's eyes can help us to see connections that would not otherwise have been visible and to find alternative ways of interpreting the meaning of the child's activity that we might otherwise have overlooked. It may help us to see our original concern in a new way and change our whole perspective on the 'problem' as we originally saw it.

Moreover, when we attempt to step out of our own frames of reference into those of a child, we need to be thinking not just about individual differences or adult–child differences but also about other relevant differences of perspective that may arise from social, cultural, linguistic, religious or gender differences between teachers and learners. As Salmon (1995: 35–6) notes:

> Our society is not, of course, homogeneous and monocultural. And for a teacher to grasp something of the personal reality experienced by a pupil from a different cultural group is not easy. It demands an imaginative understanding of young people as building their unique lives from the particular socio-cultural materials available to them, and in the process partly transforming the meanings of those materials. It means seeing features that are shared by members of that cultural group, but not being dominated by these as simple stereotypes.

Our analysis will also need to include and encompass consideration of the emotional dimension of the child's activity: how the child is feeling and how feelings shape children's responses to school experience. These further essential dimensions of the analysis will be examined in more detail in Chapter 5.

Noting the impact of feelings

But what about our own feelings? How do they influence our interpretations and judgements? The fourth questioning move involves examining how our feelings affect what we see happening and what we come to know about classroom events. Taking conscious steps to acknowledge the feelings that we are experiencing with respect to a particular child or situation that concerns or puzzles us can be a source of insight into new possibilities in two ways. It can help us to recognise how our feelings may be shaping our interpretations: perhaps predisposing us to make certain kinds of interpretations and block out others. Feelings can also be a source of insight and understanding in their own right.

When Asad's teachers spoke about what had happened in this lesson, their judgement that 'Asad had not grasped the main points' was more than just a statement about Asad's learning. It was also charged with feeling: including worry about not fulfilling their responsibilities towards Asad, disappointment that their considerable efforts had not met with greater success, and uncertainty about what else to do. Negative feelings may predispose us to make negative interpretations of the situation. Once aware of this, we can consciously and deliberately make use of the other moves, and especially the contradicting move, to try to bring to mind alternative ways of interpreting classroom events that are more positive and optimistic in their orientation.

Empathy is a form of awareness that seeks to tune into the experience of another person to give an appreciation of what the world looks and feels like from the perspective of that person. Attention to feelings, rather than to rational thought, is the means by which this is achieved. It is also possible that the feelings that children provoke in us may provide a direct source of awareness of what they are feeling. So, the disappointment experienced by Asad's teachers may have been picking up on Asad's own disappointment in failing to make sense of classroom tasks and/or in failing to please his teacher by offering an answer to her questions that would meet with her approval.

In making use of this and the other three moves so far discussed, we need to draw on all that we know about the child, the class, the situation and all the knowledge that we have acquired from experience, reading and professional training. It is this knowledge base that enables us to generate alternative meanings and possibilities beyond those that first spring to mind. However, in some circumstances we may become aware that the resources we have available are insufficient for this purpose. We may lack vital information. We may also become aware that our existing professional knowledge base needs expanding in some key respects before we would have confidence in using it to explore alternative ways of making sense of a child's responses. In my own research, for instance, I found that I simply did not have a ready-made language and set of concepts for describing the knowledge and skills in creative writing that one exceptional young writer was demonstrating in his written work.

Postponing judgement in order to find out more

To complement the four moves already discussed, therefore, a fifth move is needed which involves postponing the attempt to arrive at a conclusion, while taking steps to learn more or acquire the additional information that is felt to be essential to achieving an adequate understanding. This fifth move recognises that what we see and understand about children's learning is always shaped (and limited) by the knowledge that we have available to guide and shape our seeing. There will always be some things that we do not see, or cannot yet see, but *would become able to see* if new information or understanding were acquired. Another pair of eyes, a helpful piece of research, a new activity which reveals the child in a different light, can all help to open up new perspectives on the situation and help us to uncover previously unconsidered possibilities.

If I was Asad's teacher, I might decide that one critical piece of information that I did not yet have was what Asad had to say about his learning, both in that particular session and more generally. I would know what he had said when I had attempted to probe his understanding of the 'main points' (Figure 2.2) but I might not know how he himself felt about his work, whether he had gained a sense of achievement and success, or was left with a sense of confusion, uncertainty and failure. What were the reasons why he had not chosen to work with a partner? Was he feeling isolated and excluded by other children? Talking to Asad could help to shed fresh light on a number of hypotheses generated so far through the use of each of the first four moves, and therefore help to decide which were worth pursuing further.

I might also decide that, before proceeding further with the analysis, I wanted to observe Asad carrying out further activities, with different methods of presenting and demonstrating learning. This might help me to distinguish between difficulties in understanding and difficulties in expressing his understanding in English, and to establish patterns in his responses to learning activities of different kinds across the curriculum. These small enquiries need not be enormously time consuming – I could fit them in as part of my regular interactions with Asad – but the new information obtained would, however, play a vital role in helping me to develop a more adequate understanding of Asad's learning and establish a sounder basis from which to generate ideas for further supporting and enhancing his learning.

Towards a sound basis for action

When I have discussed Asad's story with groups of teachers, all of these questions and possibilities and more have been raised. Readers will no doubt also have been forming their own thoughts about Asad's response to this lesson, and hopefully will have found at least some of those thoughts reflected in the analysis presented here. If so, then the example will have served an important additional purpose, in enabling readers to recognise the links between the approach to thinking through teaching proposed in this book and their own ways of making sense of classroom events.

Only teachers who have close knowledge of the particular child and situation, however, would have a sense of which of these questions might be relevant to understanding the child's response on that occasion; only they would be in a position to move on from a preliminary exploration of possibilities, to a provisional conclusion regarding the meaning of the situation and the potential for further action to be taken. The purpose, at that stage, is not to attempt to come up with a full and complete understanding but simply to try to achieve sufficient *new insight* to offer a constructive way forward. Fuller understanding will develop gradually, as a consequence of translating existing insights into practice and then reflecting afresh on what might be learnt from further experience.

It is also important that the analysis makes use of all five questioning moves. Since each opens up a dimension of the situation that the others take for granted, our understanding would inevitably be partial if our analysis were to overlook routinely one or more of these different dimensions. The various moves also need to operate *together*, in interaction with one another, so that ideas arising from one are considered and checked out via other moves in a continuing dialogue (Hart 1996: 128). In this way, we ensure that emerging ideas have been thoroughly examined, so that we can have confidence in using them to inform our teaching (see Figure 2.3).

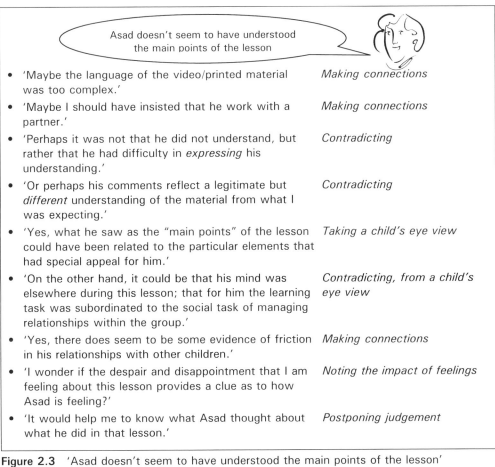

Figure 2.3 'Asad doesn't seem to have understood the main points of the lesson'

As we have seen, it is perfectly possible to think in the ways reflected in the moves spontaneously without reference to the framework – as Emer's retrospective thinking about Costas in Chapter 1 shows. As she carried out the analysis, Emer allowed her ideas to flow freely in a spontaneous, unstructured way as new thoughts about the situation occurred to her but, looking closely, we can see the moves of the framework reflected in her thinking (see Figure 2.4). Checking out newly emerging understandings in this way provides confidence that our spontaneous thinking has not overlooked important features of the situation that need to be taken into account (see Figure 2.5).

Costas didn't listen to my instructions

- 'It may actually have been difficult to hear what was said because there was a lot of noise and bustle in the room at the time.' — *Making connections*
- 'Perhaps it wasn't that he didn't listen but he *guessed* what the teacher was going to say when he saw the box.' — *Contradicting*
- 'Yes, since the game was his favourite, it may be that he heard what he wanted to hear.' — *Taking a child's eye view*
- 'I assumed that he knew that it was lunch time, but he may just have thought we were starting a new activity.' — *Contradicting from a child's eye view*
- 'If he did think he was volunteering to play a game, it was a reasonable assumption, since we do often go to the library to play games.' — *Taking a child's eye view*
- 'And also why send two people if the task was just to put the box away?' — *Making connections from a child's eye view*
- 'I recognise that I felt irritated with Costas because he had not been able to do what seemed to me to be such a simple thing. I think that this predisposed me to a negative interpretation of what was happening.' — *Noting the impact of feelings*
- 'Did Costas know what/where the "library" was?' — *Postponing judgement in order to find out more*

Figure 2.4 'Costas didn't listen to my instructions'

Questioning move:	Takes into account:
Making connections	the impact of the immediate and wider learning environment
Contradicting	our own expectations and assumptions
Taking a child's eye view	the child's meanings and agendas
Noting the impact of feelings	how our feelings shape our interpretations
Postponing judgement	the limits of what we know

Figure 2.5 Dimensions of a situation that interpretations need to take into account

These two examples illustrate how the moves work together to build meaning. The ideas generated via each move respond to ideas suggested by other moves in order to confirm, extend and challenge existing thinking. Teachers who have made use of the framework to support their analysis of classroom experience have found using the moves particularly helpful in those situations where their own thinking appeared to have run into an impasse. They found that the various different moves provided a powerful means of freeing up their thinking and opening up new possibilities. This process was at its most effective when there was the opportunity to carry out the analysis in discussion with one or more colleagues. Where teachers were working collaboratively (for example, mainstream classroom teachers with support/advisory teachers), they were able to create conditions of mutual support and stimulus that enhanced the exploration of possibilities.

Innovative thinking is a creative process. As a result of carrying out such an analysis, teachers generate ideas for increasing participation and learning that were not evident at the outset. The original interpretation, or concern, is transformed into new under-standing that can be used to inform and guide subsequent work. Sometimes (as in the case of Emer and Costas in Chapter 1) the analysis will change the teacher's perception of the problem and the child in a way that subtly changes the dynamics of the situation but does not necessarily require any specific steps to be taken on the part of the teacher. More often, it leads to new understandings that suggest particular directions for the development of practice. The teacher chooses, from the range of possibilities gener-ated, the combination of interpretations that is both illuminating and takes account of what she already knows about the child and situation. She works out how to translate her insights into specific steps for enhancing the child's participation, learning and inclusion in the activities of the whole class. She decides on particular strategies and incorporates these into her ongoing work with the class, reviewing her thinking once again in the light of the child's response.

Links with teachers' existing expertise

When the process is described in words, it no doubt seems impossibly complicated and time consuming, but in practice it need not be. It can take only minutes to carry out an analysis that can have a powerful impact on teachers' thinking and practice, as well as important consequences for children's learning, as the example of Emer and Costas in Chapter 1 illustrates. Moreover, experience of using the framework does appear to confirm that it simply makes explicit strategies which many teachers *already* use sponta-neously in the course of everyday teaching. Making them explicit enables them to be used in a more conscious and deliberate way to support the processes of review and reflection.

Trying to 'make connections', for instance, is something that we constantly do during the course of ordinary teaching, as we continuously monitor what is going on in our classrooms and make whatever adjustments we judge to be needed. If children seem unresponsive, we rapidly review a range of possibilities in order to decide what action can be taken to influence the situation positively. Is it something to do with the task content/with the mode of presentation/with the complexity of the language/some-thing going on in the dynamics of the group? Is it to do with the time of day/week or year or have they just had PE? We make a judgement based on our prior knowledge of the class and reading of the current situation, adjust accordingly and then use the children's responses as further feedback, and if necessary begin the process again.

It is also part of our expertise, as teachers, to be able to counter one reading of a situation with one or more others as a way of deciding how best to respond ('contra-dicting'). Our first reaction to a child who grins, looks nonchalant, or answers back when told off may be to think that the child does not care and is untouched by our disapproval. Yet we also know from experience that such reactions are very often defence mechanisms and provide evidence that the child *is* touched by our words, and *does* care. Recognising this, we can change our own behaviour and avoid action that might lead to confrontation.

Trying to think ourselves into the child's shoes and view the situation from that perspective is a familiar strategy for many teachers. We are not taken in by a child who is forever 'losing' or 'forgetting' his reading book, suspecting that he is probably alerting us to the fear and frustration he is experiencing in learning to read. We also try to remain open to the possibility that what at first glance appears to be a misunderstanding or a wrong answer may turn out to be an ingenious but *different* understanding from the one that we were expecting. We ask children to explain their thinking, and show their workings on paper, so that we can understand where they are coming from and engage with them on their terms.

The way that feelings affect our judgements and behaviour will, I am sure, also be readily recognised by teachers. Behaviour that prompts friendly banter on Monday morning may seem like a serious challenge to our authority on a wet Friday afternoon. Pupils' failure to cooperate with a request will tend to prompt a different response on our part depending upon whether the perpetrator is an individual or class with whom we usually get on well or not. We recognise that such differences of perception are partly a product of our own states of mind, and try to correct imbalances that we are aware of in our treatment and perception of pupils.

Even postponing judgement, because we recognise that we lack adequate information or resources, is a strategy which will be familiar to teachers, in spite of its seeming impracticality in the busy world of school and classroom. Teachers are very aware of the dangers of the 'self-fulfilling prophecy' and are conscious of the need to keep an open mind about individuals, particularly on first meeting. Many teachers also try to teach in a way that is genuinely open-ended, by tuning into children's purposes and thinking in order to discover what help they need in order to learn, rather than pre-defining their paths to learning.

In *Beyond Special Needs* (Hart 1996: 11) I argued that innovative thinking makes use not only of the same expertise but also the same knowledge which teachers bring every day to the complex task of classroom teaching. All experienced teachers have extensive knowledge about the dynamics of teaching and learning, and about what makes a difference to how children behave and to how well they learn in school. We draw on this knowledge constantly, both consciously and intuitively, in planning lessons, in interpreting what is happening minute-by-minute in classrooms and especially in reviewing what happened in order to plan future lessons.

This knowledge provides a powerful resource for the interpretation of classroom events but the circumstances of classroom teaching do not allow us to exploit its possibilities fully. There is far more knowledge stored in the filing cabinets of the mind than we can ever make spontaneous use of in the course of ordinary teaching. The five questioning moves that support the process of innovative thinking are the means by which we marshall this knowledge and use it flexibly and imaginatively to support us in the vital processes of reviewing our judgements and practices and drawing out the implications for future work.

PART TWO

In the second part of the book, I examine each of the questioning moves that make up the framework in more detail. Although I have suggested that the power of the framework lies in making use of all the moves flexibly, simultaneously, and in interaction with one another, it may be helpful, initially, to consider each in isolation in order to explore what is distinctive about the perspective that each move has to offer.

The three main purposes of this part of the book are:

- to enable readers to develop their understanding of what each move entails, and to make links between the thinking processes described and their own active ways of making sense of what happens in their classrooms;
- to encourage readers to recall and review their own reservoir of relevant knowledge, by reviewing ideas drawn from the literature and from practical experience that support the functioning of each move;
- to illustrate, through concrete examples, the active part that the ideas of others – and in particular ideas derived from reading and research – can play in assisting, extending and enhancing the reflective process.

A separate chapter is devoted to each of the five questioning moves, each presenting a brief summary of what the move entails, an elaboration of the questions which it encourages teachers to ask and an exploration of issues that it might be relevant to consider.

CHAPTER 3
Making connections

> This move involves *exploring connections* that might be made between children's classroom responses and the immediate or wider learning environment. We ask ourselves: 'How are features of the context influencing children's learning and behaviour? What, in this situation, might have contributed to this response?'

Making connections is something that I believe many teachers do automatically, as part of the process of monitoring what is happening minute-by-minute in the classroom. If the children seem restless while listening to a story, for instance, we speedily review some possible connections with the immediate learning environment to decide what action to take. Is the room becoming too stuffy? Have they been sitting still too long? Do seating arrangements need to be altered? Was enough done initially to engage the children's interests? What could be done now to generate interest and excitement about what will happen? We each have our own in-built checklist of possibilities (acquired through experience, through our professional training and through reading) that helps us to interpret what is going on in our classrooms and to adjust teaching continually in the light of the feedback provided by children's responses.

What children learn and how they behave in school are influenced by many, complex interacting features of school and classroom life, including:

- relationships with teachers and peers
- expectations of teachers and peers
- curriculum content, structure, balance, relevance
- teaching styles, methods
- nature, structure and sequencing of learning tasks
- teaching resources, materials and equipment
- physical conditions: size, shape of classrooms, proximity of other children
- physical environment: displays, organisation of tables, desks, etc.
- classroom language, styles of interaction, questioning, instruction, explanation
- classroom organisation, management, rules, routines
- modes of grouping, group composition
- modes and methods of assessment and feedback on work
- organisation of learning support
- pastoral support
- liaison with parents
- overall school ethos and messages of value.

In planning, we automatically draw on this knowledge to design learning experiences and conditions that will promote the kinds of learning that we seek to foster. We put careful thought into the organisation of the physical environment; into the design of tasks, the materials to be used, and the sequence of activities intended to develop particular concepts and understandings. We make careful decisions about the size and composition of groupings to create the most productive working units, consciously working at building positive relationships with individuals and within class groups, aware of the important part that relationships play in enabling – or constraining – learning.

When we make connections, as part of the retrospective analysis of teaching, we draw on the same knowledge used in planning and in managing our moment-by-moment classroom decision-making, using it this time to help us to make sense of, and learn from, evidence of children's engagement with classroom learning activities. The purpose is to try to identify connections between children's classroom responses and features of the learning context, so that we can use these to reach a fuller understanding of what is happening, and to suggest possible ways of intervening to adjust or change features of the situation in order to enhance learning.

Some examples of the process of making connections have already been examined. In Chapter 1, for instance, Emer's review of the circumstances surrounding Costas's apparent failure to listen to instructions made connections with:

- the noise and bustle of a class clearing up that may have affected his ability to hear what was actually said;
- possible ambiguities or previously unacknowledged complexities in the way that she had phrased her request and instructions about what needed to be done;
- how her body language and tone of voice might have affected Costas's response to her question when she found the two boys standing outside the door.

In Chapter 2, we looked in some detail at how Asad's perceived difficulties in grasping the main points of the lesson might be connected to features of the learning context, including:

- relationships with other children in the class
- the lesson content
- the abstract nature of the task
- how the task was presented and how its purpose negotiated with the children
- features of the learning materials and resources used
- features of classroom organisation
- Asad's physical positioning and proximity to the teacher.

These connections were made by shifting the focus of attention from the child to the learning context and implicitly asking 'What, in this situation, might have influenced the child's response?' In Costas's case, Emer was implicitly asking herself 'What might have made it difficult for Costas to hear, internalise and follow my instructions?' Similarly, in making connections between Asad's perceived difficulties and features of the immediate learning environment, we were implicitly asking 'What might have made it difficult for Asad to engage successfully with this task?'

Making connections helps to safeguard the interests of children by ensuring that learners' responses (Costas's 'failure to listen to instructions' and Asad's 'failure to understand the main points of the lesson') are viewed as outcomes of the complex interaction between learners and the learning opportunities provided, rather than purely as a failure of effort or intellect on the part of the child. It also empowers teachers because, when we make connections with the immediate context that were not obvious before, these new insights suggest ways of intervening to aid children's participation and learning that might not otherwise have come to our attention.

In this chapter, I use some further examples to illustrate the process of making connections with features of the immediate and wider learning environment. Although the focus of the analysis is always upon the immediate situation, it is important to consider connections that extend beyond the individual classroom. In order to develop a fuller understanding of what is happening in the immediate situation, we may need to take account of features of the overall school context, and indeed features of children's out-of-school experience in the home and community. In making these wider connections, the teacher's purpose is always to use them to try to identify ways of enhancing learning *within* the immediate situation, not to find explanations for what is happening which places learners' responses beyond the teacher's control. Teachers do not, of course, have unlimited power, but it is our responsibility to ensure that we are able to exploit as fully as possible the scope that *is* available to us for improving children's learning and achievements, within the inevitable limiting pressures, constraints and external influences.

Making connections at classroom level

Although both the examples we have examined so far have been concerned with individual children, events that strike teachers as worthy of further thought may equally well refer to more generalised impressions, such as (for example) pupils' apparent difficulties in recalling ideas previously learnt, patterns of classroom interaction where particular pupils dominate, or difficulties in sustaining productive talk in small groups.

The latter was often a focus for reflective analysis in my own teaching, when I was experimenting with developing collaborative group work in integrated humanities (Hart and Scott 1987; Hart 1989). Newly prepared activities were rarely entirely successful, because it was impossible to foresee, at the point of planning, every possible problem or confusion that might arise. The less well-judged the activities, the more the noise and frustration levels would rise, and the more dependent children would become upon my support to help them to sort out their difficulties. Sometimes, I would come out of lessons feeling completely drained by the demands of so many pupils apparently needing help simultaneously. This was, needless to say, quite contrary to my intentions, since I was using collaborative group work as a means of freeing children from reliance upon the teacher as fount of all knowledge, as a means of enabling them to make sense of curriculum ideas in their own terms. Since I had strong educational reasons to want to pursue the potential of this approach, it was imperative to analyse these not-so-successful lessons in order to see what might be learnt that would help to foster more productive group learning.

During the first year that I tried working in this way, I found that there were many issues at the level of general class management that needed to be sorted out in order to enable pupils to work in self-sustaining groups. There also needed to be some explicit negotiation with pupils about the value of discussion and group work, and steps taken to establish an ethos in which pupils' own knowledge and experience was valued as a resource for classroom learning. By the second year, ways of working had been established where these issues were largely resolved; yet there were still occasions when the group work would break down, when I would find myself working flat out in order to try to salvage the situation. On these occasions, it was essential to review the distinctive features of those particular lessons, in order to see what might have contributed to the breakdown of effective collaborative working.

To illustrate the process of making connections at classroom level, I shall draw on this personal experience (no doubt also familiar to others) and consider some of the connections that might be worth pursuing in this case. What might make it difficult for pupils to sustain productive, collaborative work on some occasions but not others?

The appropriateness of classroom tasks

One obvious area to focus upon is the nature of the tasks or activities provided. What was it about the particular tasks and activities provided on those occasions that made pupils unable to work things out for themselves and solve problems together? Were the tasks simply too difficult for the majority of the class? Decisions made (with due thought) at the point of planning can sometimes turn out to have been very wide of the mark when translated into practice in the classroom. This is not as surprising as it might seem, because many different factors go to make up 'task appropriateness', as the following examples seek to illustrate.

Context and meaning of classroom tasks

Perhaps, rather than making cognitive demands that were beyond the reach of the majority of the class, the problem was that the tasks were conceived and presented in a way which did not call forth the full extent of pupils' existing competences. Margaret Donaldson (1978), for example, designed some ingenious experiments to show that children of four who were thought to be too young to be able to 'decentre' were able to do so when the problem to be solved was reformulated in a way that made 'human sense' to them. Piaget's 'three mountains' problem required children to form a mental representation of what the model of the three mountains looked like from other than their own point of view. When Donaldson and colleagues transformed this problem into a story about a little boy hiding from a policeman, the children were in fact able to put themselves into the position of the policeman and say whether or not the little boy was hidden or not from the policeman's point of view.

Although Donaldson's work has itself been questioned by other researchers (e.g. Adey and Shayer 1994), one undoubted contribution it has made has been to alert us to think carefully about how features of the design of tasks may affect children's response and therefore give us misleading information about the limits of their existing capabilities. Donaldson's work reminds us to look carefully at the nature of the task, the language and instructions in order to see how meaningful they are to children. What may be needed is not to make the task simpler (and thereby possibly limit unnecessarily children's opportunities for learning), but to look for ways of embedding the same demands in a context that makes more human sense and is therefore able to call forth the full extent of children's existing competences.

A similar argument is made, with respect to the education of bilingual children, by Frederikson and Cline (1996), drawing on the work of Jim Cummins (Cummins and Swain 1986). When bilingual children struggle with classroom tasks, we may interpret this as meaning that the tasks are conceptually too complex and offer them less conceptually demanding material, when actually what is needed is to provide more contextual support. To clarify the argument, they refer to Cummins's two-dimensional model of language proficiency, where one continuum represents the 'context-embeddedness' or 'disembeddedness' of tasks, and the other the degree of conceptual demand ranging from high demand to low demand (see Figure 3.1).

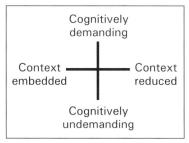

Figure 3.1 Cummins's two-dimensional model

On the horizontal dimension, context-embedded tasks would be those where language was embedded in a meaningful context, where visual support material was available, and where there were also cues to meaning from gesture and expression. Context-reduced tasks, on the other hand, are those that provide only linguistic cues to meaning. As an example, Frederikson and Cline (1996: 14) explain that if a child is asked to read the sentence 'I like to skip' as one of a series of unconnected sentences in a reading test, this would be an example of a 'context reduced' task. If the child were asked to read the same sentence just after it had been written to their dictation under a picture which they had drawn, this would be an example of written language use embedded in a context that was meaningful to the child.

The vertical dimension indicates the level of cognitive demand placed on the child by language used in any particular task or situation. Cognitive demand depends upon both inherent qualities of the task and on characteristics of individual children, such as the familiarity and acceptability of the task to the child. Classroom tasks that are, in Cummins's terms, located in the top, right-hand quadrant present difficulties to bilingual learners that could be overcome not by reducing conceptual demand but by embedding those demands in more meaningful and supportive contexts (top left-hand quadrant).

Textual difficulties

As well as looking closely at features of the design, presentation and organisation of tasks, it would be important also to consider possible barriers to task engagement and learning that may be bound up with the language of any printed materials used. Ideas that are perfectly accessible to children presented in other forms may become inaccessible due to features of the language and layout of printed texts. It is often not until children have actually used classroom materials for particular purposes that the problems they may pose to children become apparent to fluent adult readers, and particularly to teachers who are subject specialists.

I found the work of Katherine Perera (1979; 1984) particularly helpful in providing a breakdown of the kinds of problems that can occur at word, sentence and discourse levels (see Figure 3.2). Becoming more aware of the difficulties that texts can present to

---

Word level

1. *Familiar words presented in unfamiliar ways*, e.g.
   'The camel *caravans* trudged the old *silk roads* between the ancient cities of Constantinople and Peking' and 'Priests generally *arose* at a later period in time when there were special holy buildings called temples'. Children will understand the meanings of the words 'caravan', 'road' and 'arose' but the familiar meanings that they assign to them will not enable them to interpret these passages appropriately.

2. *Technical vocabulary*
   • Confusion may arise from familiar words used with a 'specialist' meaning, e.g. 'solution' in Science, 'volume' in Mathematics.
   • Perera distinguishes between technical words which are a necessary part of the language and concepts of the discipline and 'jargon'.
   • As a rule of thumb, the more technical terms a text contains, the more difficult it will be to read

Sentence level

1. *Sentence structures which occur infrequently in spoken language*
   e.g. *'That the level of the sea rises and falls twice in every 24 hours* is obvious to anyone at the seaside' (unfamiliar in speech).

2. *Difficulties created by absence of intonation cues*
   e.g. 'He feared *the Saracens might conquer his country too*.' The absence of 'that' might lead weaker readers to think the sentence reads 'He feared the Saracens' and then to be confused by 'might conquer'.

3. *Difficulties created by long grammatical consitutents*
   e.g. *'A* SYSTEM *in which nobles are given estates of land in exchange for the use of their soldiers* IS CALLED feudal rule.' The reader has to hold 18 words in memory before reaching the verb. Perera quotes research which indicates that 'average' 6-year-old readers can retain 4–5 words in short-term memory, 9-year-olds 8–10 words and 12-year-olds 10–13 words. Slower readers have greater difficulty because their speed of processing may be too slow to take in whole grammatical constituents.

Discourse level

Readers may understand all the words and all the sentence structures in a passage, yet still not be able to grasp the overall meaning. They also need to understand the overall discourse structure, the way that ideas are put together to create meaning. They need to process information provided by markers such as 'in addition', 'similarly', 'furthermore', 'therefore', 'consequently', 'however', 'on the contrary', in order to follow the author's line of argument and understand the structure of the whole. Meaning may also depend upon readers being able to interpret graphs and diagrams alongside text.

Figure 3.2 Difficulties presented by school texts (adapted from Perera 1979, all examples quoted are from published school texts)

learners can help us to refine the qualities of texts and forms of presentation of learning materials that we produce ourselves. Being forewarned about likely difficulties in commercially produced materials can also help us to plan strategies to help children to tackle difficulties successfully. The most helpful approach may not be to simplify the texts themselves, but rather to encourage active approaches to engaging with their meanings (for example, underlining or highlighting key ideas in different ways, and using these markers to explore the relationships between ideas and the meaning of the text as whole).

Further insight into the way that classroom language can create barriers to learning is provided by Hull (1985). As part of a year-long study of classroom language in secondary schools, he looked closely at the use of school textbooks in order to understand what led to the difficulties experienced by many pupils in reading them. He noted some of the intrinsic qualities of texts which may create obstacles to engagement: for example the flat, voiceless form in which most information texts used in school are written which does not reach out and draw the reader in. He also examined how page layouts make assumptions about how the page is to be read, showing that what are perceived as 'difficulties' in reading may be due to the fact that readers do not know how to 'read' the layout.

As an example, he analyses the text shown in Figure 3.3. The reader needs to know that the words in the box are used to complete the sentences, that they need to be combined in order to do so (keeps, water, head). Although, in the layout code, the pictures are intended to function as clues, in fact you need the text in order to interpret the pictures. As Hull points out:

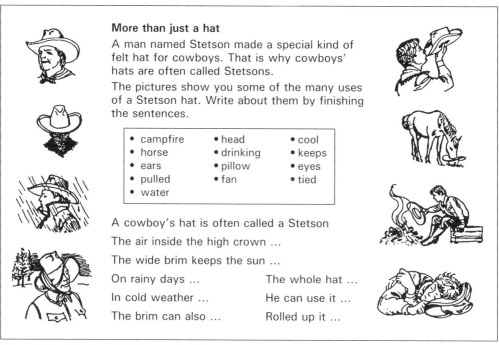

More than just a hat

A man named Stetson made a special kind of felt hat for cowboys. That is why cowboys' hats are often called Stetsons.

The pictures show you some of the many uses of a Stetson hat. Write about them by finishing the sentences.

• campfire	• head	• cool
• horse	• drinking	• keeps
• ears	• pillow	• eyes
• pulled	• fan	• tied
• water		

A cowboy's hat is often called a Stetson

The air inside the high crown ...

The wide brim keeps the sun ...

On rainy days ...   The whole hat ...

In cold weather ...   He can use it ...

The brim can also ...   Rolled up it ...

Figure 3.3   Reading the layout of a classroom text

The obscurity of the pictures' meanings is such that text is necessary to interpret them; pupils need the answer to understand the clue. Thus, the quaint picture of what looks like an old lady's hat (bottom left) needs 'in cold weather' for it to be understood. The first picture is so neutral as to make it hard to juxtapose specifically with 'high crown', just as 'the whole hat ...' could be completed with reference to any of the eight pictures.   (Hull 1985: 98)

The 'difficulties' presented by the text, Hull argues, are not just intrinsic to the text. If the use of this exercise were linked to other work, such as a project on cowboys, reading a western, writing a story, then this would provide a stronger context which would make the text itself more 'readable'. The ideas and associated language would have a more immediate history, and perhaps a more personal engagement which would assist in deciphering the 'puzzle-page language' (Hull 1985: 98). When exercises are presented as discrete tasks, with no context other than that provided by the page itself, readers are cut off from their own language and their knowledge resources which give language meaning. They are unable to gather *their* thoughts and *their* language.

Hull's argument, then, is that in order to address difficulties in reading school texts, we need to do more than look carefully at the texts themselves. Difficulties are produced 'by the structure of relations in school between text, knowledge and the pupils' world' (p. 198). Texts will not become more accessible by being simplified, if this 'structure of relations' remains unchanged (indeed attempts at 'simplification' can sometimes make them more difficult to read).

Using these ideas to help understand why children might experience difficulties in sustaining collaborative group work in some situations rather than others would lead not just to close examination of the texts themselves but also how they were expected to be used by pupils in a particular lesson as a resource for learning. It would be important to look carefully at issues of layout and consider what children needed to know and do in order to 'read' the layout effectively. It would also prompt some more careful consideration of the 'structure of relations', in a given lesson, between the text, the knowledge to be learnt, and the pupils' world. Were enough opportunities made available for children to bring their own subjective meanings to bear on the text, to interpret it in their own terms? What could have been done to improve their opportunities to do so?

Scaffolding classroom tasks

In addition to questions about the nature and uses of printed materials, there is always a need to think carefully about the active role played by the teacher in supporting and enabling learning. When analysing a situation where children seemed to be in need of constant help, it would be important to look back at the pattern and nature of interactions with children to see if there was anything significant about the way that time was divided up on this occasion. It would be useful to think, too, about what the many interactions with children accomplished and about how these interactions affected their sense of competence and control over their work. Was the right kind of help provided at the right time? How do we determine what kinds of help are needed and when to provide them? How do we make those judgements, and manage time, with thirty children simultaneously?

The notion of scaffolding is used by Bruner (1985) to represent the special qualities of guidance or collaboration that teachers provide to enable learners to move on from an existing stage of understanding or competence to a new one. Scaffolding is employed by teachers in order to enable pupils to carry out, with help, tasks that they are not yet able to do independently. Gradually, pupils are enabled to take over control of the whole operation themselves. Maybin, Mercer and Stierer (1992) analysed transcripts of teachers' conversations with students, exploring the forms of scaffolding that teachers adopt in particular circumstances, the reasons for them, and their impact on pupils' learning. In a primary classroom, for example, children were working on a task which involved working out a classification key for sea shells. Two boys were stuck and appealed to their teacher for help. Maybin *et al.* (1992) describe the teacher's intervention as follows:

> He tries to draw out from the boys ideas (for example, the variable of 'colour') which he knows will take them along productive paths to a solution. He gives them some feedback on their suggestions, pointing out weaknesses where they exist. He tries to help them adopt a suitably detached or 'decentred' perspective on the problem by pointing out that relative terms (like 'dark') won't work in the circumstances in which other people will use their key. On this occasion, we see pupils making progress with teacher support: by the end of the sequence they have, with his help, discovered a way of distinguishing the shells in question.
>
> (Maybin *et al.* 1992: 191)

The concept of scaffolding can, as Maybin *et al.* suggest, provide a useful analytical tool to help gain greater understanding of teaching and learning. Although it is unlikely that teachers will be able to remember the detail of their interactions with pupils after the event, the concept of scaffolding may help to achieve a more conscious and critical awareness of what we are trying to do in our work with pupils, of the range of possibilities open to us, and of the impact of what we do on pupils' subsequent learning.

The potential scope of the task

In this section, we have examined in some detail various connections that might be made with features of the immediate learning environment, when seeking to understand why pupils might have difficulty in sustaining productive collaborative work in some situations rather than others. All have been related to the 'appropriateness' of the particular tasks and activities provided, in order to illustrate the complexity of the issues that are potentially worthy of consideration in just this one area. There are, of course, many other factors that also affect task appropriateness which it would be relevant to consider. A text might be linguistically appropriate, for example, in the sense that the learners have the skills to tackle it independently; but the content and style of presentation might be inappropriate to children's interests, age or social maturity. Equally, a task which makes seemingly appropriate cognitive demands might be inaccessible to some pupils because it makes assumptions about features of shared cultural experience which are not in fact shared by those learners.

A group of experienced teachers pooled their knowledge of the many different dimensions that go to make up the 'appropriateness' of classroom learning activities. They then turned these into questions that could be used as a stimulus to thinking in the process of review (see Figure 3.4).

Is the task appropriate:
- in terms of the conceptual demands which it makes?
- in terms of the knowledge/experience/skills which it assumes?
- in terms of the language/reading/writing demands which it makes?
- in terms of its mode of presentation (concrete, practical, abstract)?
- in relation to the age/social maturity/peer identity of the learners?
- in relation to the identified needs of learners?
- in relation to learners' cultural backgrounds?
- in the sense that the learners understand the purpose?
- in the sense that the task and its outcomes matter to the learners?
- in the sense that the learners understand what they have to do?
- in the sense that it fits into a coherent set of experiences?
- in the clarity of its presentation and instructions (verbal, textual, visual)?
- given the amount and timing of teacher intervention/other forms of support?
- given the way that it is structured (for individual work, group work)?
- given the composition/size of the group?
- given the learners' interests and relevances?
- in that it provides a sense of achievement?
- in the sense that it provides the opportunity for the learner to make sense of the activity and develop it in his or her own way?

Figure 3.4   Is the task appropriate ...?

While the list illustrates the complexity of the task facing teachers in their endeavour to create learning experiences that are appropriate for a class of thirty diverse individuals, it is not intended to make teaching seem impossibly daunting. Used at the review stage, it provides a set of prompts to help teachers keep in mind the many different dimensions of classroom tasks that may affect pupils' responses, and use these to search out ways of enhancing participation and learning.

Making connections beyond the immediate context

As well as making connections between children's responses and features of the immediate classroom context, it is often important, too, to look for connections beyond the individual classroom, and consider how what happens in the immediate situation might be connected to features of overall school organisation and structure. Two of the Enfield teachers (Penny and Lesley) found themselves making such connections, as they pursued their concerns about a particular Year 7 pupil, Ayse, who never seemed really to engage with classroom tasks. While they were trying to find out more about Ayse's experiences of school learning, one of them (Penny) negotiated an opportunity to follow Ayse around for a day at school in order to see if she did engage more fully in other lessons.

Penny was genuinely taken aback to discover how demanding and confusing she herself found the sequence of different lessons, not just with their different topics, but with the different expectations and different systems of management, marking and feedback that teachers used. The experience brought home to her what considerable feats of orientation are required of a pupil to be alert and ready to learn in each of these disconnected learning experiences following rapidly upon one another. Although most teachers do, as a matter of course, include activities to help students to recall and reconnect with ideas discussed the last time that they met, Penny's observations made her appreciate how much more remote that previous occasion must seem in the student's mind than the teacher's (given that the teacher has planned and prepared the overall sequence of activities); and how important it is therefore, at the start of lessons, that activities do actively engage all students in reformulating the knowledge that is a prerequisite for learning in the current lesson.

As a result of this day's shadowing, Penny saw a possible connection between Ayse's perceived 'lack of involvement' in English lessons and the compartmentalised nature of the secondary school curriculum. Obviously, this was not something that she could change directly. Nevertheless, once the connection has been acknowledged, there *are* things that teachers can do in their classrooms to maximise the ease and swiftness with which students can tune into the ideas to be explored in the lesson. We can also be more sympathetic to those experiencing difficulties in doing so (some may have just had to abandon work in which they were deeply engrossed and would have been keen to continue with). Bearing this in mind, we can keep searching for ways of strengthening links between lessons in students' minds and a sense of the whole topic (for example through developing concept maps or mind maps) to facilitate re-engagement.

Penny and Lesley tell the full story of their work with Ayse in Chapter 9. This particular incident provides a useful illustration of how looking beyond the walls of individual classrooms and individual teachers' practices to features of the overall school context can help us to reach a fuller understanding of pupils' responses in particular lesson. As the Elton Report (DES 1989) stresses, this may be especially important with respect to understanding pupils' behaviour.

> A few of the submissions we received took the view that bad behaviour is always entirely the fault of pupils. We reject this view. No pupil is an island. Every incident has a range of immediate and longer term causes. Events in the classroom are influenced by a complex mixture of expectations, attitudes, regulations, policies and laws which are shaped by forces at work in the classroom, the school, the local community and society as a whole.   (DES 1989: 64)

The report provides a useful analysis of features of the overall school context that can make a difference to how pupils respond and how they behave. Although individual teachers cannot single-handedly effect change at a whole-school level, they may need to appreciate factors at work at that level in order to see what realistically might be done to enhance attitudes and engagement within their own teaching.

One of the areas identified for consideration by the report is the impact of schools' grouping systems upon pupils' learning and behaviour. Although the current trend is towards the introduction of more ability-based grouping (DfEE 1997a), there is a strong tradition of research in the sociological literature which has traced the negative effects that ability grouping systems can have upon teachers' expectations and pedagogy, and upon learners' attitudes to learning and to school (e.g. Jackson 1964; Hargreaves 1967; Keddie 1971; Lacey 1970; Ball 1981). In a recent study of different approaches to mathematics teaching (Boaler 1997), students were interviewed about features of their mathematical experiences which affected their achievements. Boaler argues that a number of the features that they identified as causing them to become disaffected about mathematics were intrinsically linked to setting.

All of the Year 11 students bar one (24 in total) expressed strong preferences for mixed ability teaching. This was because setting, for many of the students, meant one or more of:

- a lack of understanding when the pace of lessons was too fast
- boredom when the pace of lessons was too slow
- anxiety created by the competition and pressures of setted environments
- disaffection related to the restricted opportunities they faced; and
- perceived discrimination in setting decisions.   (Boaler 1997: 581)

Although there is no conclusive evidence to support particular approaches to grouping (Hallam and Toutounji 1998), what is clear from research is that systems of grouping do have an important impact, for better or worse, upon pupils' attitudes and achievements. Of course, school policies on grouping depend upon the agreement of groups of staff, and so are not susceptible to change by individuals. Nevertheless, there *are* things that teachers can do to mitigate the negative effects and enhance the positive benefits of whatever system is currently in use.

Connections with out-of-school experience

The search for connections between what is happening in our classrooms and the wider learning environment also needs to include pupils' out-of-school experiences, using these to shed light on how pupils respond in the classroom and to generate ideas for supporting and improving their learning further. In this area, ideas drawn from literature and research can be of particular relevance and value because researchers have the means to gain access to pupils' out-of-school experiences not ordinarily available to teachers.

Tizard and Hughes (1984), for example, studied the language used by a small sample of four-year-old girls. They tape-recorded the children talking at home with their parents and carers, and at nursery school with their teachers and assistants. Their comparison of children's language and patterns of interaction at home and at school showed up some important discrepancies. A striking contrast was found, for example, between the children's use of language at home and at school, and these differences were most marked for the 'working-class' children. At school, many of the children gave monosyllabic replies to questions and took little part in conversations. Yet at home they showed themselves to be able to use complex language competently for a wide range of purposes.

One of a number of possible reasons suggested by Tizard and Hughes to account for these differences in language behaviour at home and at school was the different pattern of interaction noted between teachers and children and between the children and their parents. Whereas at home, talk was used more collaboratively, with adults and children engaged in a shared agenda, often initiated by the child, in school the teacher's questions and agenda more often prevailed. This seemed to reduce the children's sense of having a contribution to make to the conversation. The 'middle-class' group of girls was apparently less affected by these differences in conversational style.

Such differences between talk at home and at school have been confirmed by other influential studies (e.g. Wells 1986). These are very important findings, because they show that features of the context affect children's ability and willingness to make use of the full extent of their existing linguistic competences. If we do not take account of how children's responses are influenced by features of the context, we may seriously underestimate children's linguistic capabilities. Tizard and Hughes noticed, for example, that in their interactions with children, the teachers in this particular study:

> made less frequent use of language for complex purposes when addressing the working-class girls than the middle-class girls. They were more likely to initiate conversations with working-class girls by questioning them, and their 'cognitive demands' were pitched at a lower level. They gave a more restricted range of information to the working-class children. They were less likely to ask the working-class children for descriptions, and more likely to ask them intellectually easy questions concerned with labelling objects and naming their attributes (e.g. 'What's that called? What colour is it?').   (1984: 222)

Research findings such as these could be of critical importance to a teacher who, in reviewing her teaching, is thinking about how best to meet the language development needs of those children who seem least disposed to express their ideas in talk. Awareness of them could help to ensure that judgements about children's existing linguistic competences take account of the influence of the context. Action could be directed towards discovering what changes might be made, for instance, in styles of interaction, modes of questioning, contexts of interaction (one to one, small group, whole class), or patterns governing the initiation of conversation, in order to draw children out and give them confidence in expressing their ideas.

More recently, the work of Eve Gregory (e.g. 1993; 1994) has been salutary in providing insights into how the gulf between experiences at home and at school can create difficulties for children. She tells the story of Tony, a young Chinese boy, who started school full of enthusiasm, according to his teacher, but whose behaviour completely changed over the next few months (Gregory 1993). He ceased smiling, became (in her words) 'difficult to get through to', threw away his drawings and increasingly avoided sharing books with his teacher. In response to her concern, his teacher visited Tony's parents in their home and discovered the very different expectations and assumptions about reading held by Tony's parents and which he had therefore brought with him to school. These differences included different perceptions of the purposes of reading; different views of the learning process, and of the part played by books in learning to read and write; and different expectations of children's role in the learning process. It was by coming to appreciate how these differences might help to explain Tony's reactions in school, that she was able to see what more she might do in a school context to help Tony to develop as a reader, building on and developing his existing skills and understandings.

Summary

Making connections is *one* essential part of the process of reflective analysis. In searching out connections that might be made with the immediate and wider learning environment, we draw selectively upon all that we know about the pupils, the situation and what makes a difference to pupils' attitudes and engagement with school learning, and bring this to bear on the detail of what happened in a particular teaching session. We look for possible connections with the immediate context (how learning was affected by the nature of the tasks, resources, relationships, groupings, etc.), with the wider school context (e.g. grouping systems, messages of value, curriculum organisation) and children's out-of-school experience. The purpose is always to search out possibilities – arising from the analysis – for developing and improving our teaching which will benefit individuals, particular groups or the whole class.

Although the process makes use of the same knowledge that we use in planning, fresh classroom evidence stimulates us to use our existing knowledge in new ways, generating new ideas and understandings that have not previously occurred to us. We thus *develop* our knowledge base through *actively using* it to explore the meaning of what is happening in our classrooms. We can also develop it – and extend the range of connections that we are able to make – through access to research and literature which offers new insight into the relationship between children's learning and features of classroom learning environments beyond those we are already able to make from within our existing resources. This chapter has illustrated how the published work of teachers and researchers can be used as a vital supplementary source of ideas which serves both to remind us of what we already know and to enrich, extend and challenge our own existing knowledge and understanding.

'Making connections' is just one way of generating new ideas and possibilities in the process of thinking through teaching. Even if some very powerful ideas emerge when we look at our practice from this point of view, we would base any developments on a very partial view of the situation if we only examined it from this perspective – many other important features of the situation would be left unexplored. These other features are reflected in the other four questioning moves, and are examined in more detail in the following chapters.

CHAPTER 4
Contradicting

This move involves *taking a fresh look at the evidence* upon which an interpretation is based in order to see if we can *come up with contrasting meanings*. Doing this helps to tease out the norms and expectations underlying the original interpretation. Becoming aware of them allows us to examine them afresh and to explore the practical implications of alternative readings. We ask ourselves: 'Have I got this wrong? How might this situation be understood differently?'

The meaning of classroom events does not present itself to us ready-made but is constructed by us though complex processes of interpretation. Meanings depend not just upon the actual events unfolding before our eyes, but also upon what *we* bring to the interpretive task: the particular knowledge, experience, values, beliefs and expectations that we use to make sense of what occurs. Yet, once made, our interpretations tend to take on an external reality, independent from our own acts of meaning-making (e.g. 'Asad has not grasped the main points', 'Costas did not listen to instructions', 'the children were unable to work independently'). It is easy to lose sight of the fact that these *are* just interpretations, and consequently that there may be other ways of making sense of the same set of events.

The second questioning move, contradicting, involves taking a devil's advocate position with respect to our perceptions and judgements: challenging existing interpretations by looking for different ways of interpreting the same evidence which cast the meaning in a contrasting light. It is based on the conviction that 'different constructions are always possible – there are always other, possibly more fruitful ways of looking at things' (Salmon 1995: 24). Once we have construed a situation in a particular way, however, it can be very difficult to see it differently. Readers will no doubt have come across 'trick' pictures where the same configurations on the page can be seen, for example, as both a stereotypical old woman and a beautiful young woman. Even when we have seen both pictures, and know both are there, it is still very difficult to make a conscious switch between them – the one we are currently seeing blocks out the other. It is hardly surprising, then, that in the much more complicated acts of seeing in which we engage in classrooms, the switch can be even more difficult. Yet it is important, in children's interests, to make the conscious effort needed to do so. An alternative interpretation can put a very different gloss on the situation and suggest a very different course of action, as we have seen in some of the examples already examined in the book (see Table 4.1).

In this chapter, I examine the process of contradicting in more detail using some examples to illustrate how a consideration of contrasting readings of the same situation

Table 4.1 Examples of contrasting interpretations

Original interpretation	Evidence	Contrasting interpretations
1. Asad has not grasped the main points of the lesson	The actual words that Asad said in response to his teacher's question, and features of the context in which the exchange occurred.	• Asad had difficulty in expressing his understanding • Asad had a legitimate but different understanding from what his teacher was expecting.
2. Costas did not listen to the instructions	Costas is at the classroom door 5 mins after his teacher sent him on an errand.	• Costas did not hear the instructions because of all the noise and bustle in the room. • Costas read the non-verbal features of the situation and inferred that he was being invited to play a game.

can help to tease out the expectations and values underlying an expression of dissatisfaction or concern. I explore why it is important for children that we should be prepared to reconsider the norms, expectations and views of learning and achievement underlying our judgements. I also look at the commonalities between contradicting and the technique of 'reframing' (Molnar and Lindquist 1989) used to assist teachers in responding constructively to challenging behaviour.

The power of contrasting readings

A striking example of the power of alternative interpretations to change our perspective upon a situation is provided by a primary teacher, Ros Frost, who observed a child in her class as part of an assignment on an in-service course. Jamie's behaviour had for some time been causing her considerable grief and stress, and she wanted to take a fresh look at the situation. Ros found that just taking time to look and think, during a period when another teacher was taking her class, allowed her to see alternative ways of interpreting Jamie's behaviour that she was convinced she would have registered as further examples of his 'distractedness', 'disruptiveness' or 'work avoidance strategies' under the usual pressured conditions of classroom life. Ros set these differences out as shown in Table 4.2.

One notable feature of these interpretations is that *both* sets were products of Ros's system of values, beliefs and assumptions about children, teaching and learning, and about what counts as worthwhile activity and appropriate behaviour. Both were interpretations of the evidence consistent with this value system, but they drew selectively on different norms and values in each case. For example, Ros's concern about what she perceived as Jamie's lack of concentration and disturbance of others reflects a belief that good learning requires sustained concentration. Against these criteria, talking or getting up and moving around, then, is interpreted as a sign that concentration has been

Table 4.2 Alternative interpretations of Jamie's behaviour

Time	Action	Relaxed interpretation	Stressed interpretation
9.32	Talks when working	Helpful automatic self-expression	Disturbing concentration of others
	Joking	Values friends and humour	Lack of concentration
9.35	Visits friend's table	Needs to relate to others	Disturbing concentration of others
	Asks politely for something	I may have missed this good behaviour from across the room	
	Sharpening pencil	I forgot to organise the helpers	Work avoidance tactic
	'Wooden Willy' action	J's humour; he's happy	Inappropriate behaviour
	Tells friend colour of eyes	Helping his friend	Lack of concentration
9.41	Propels rubber using ruler with description of mechanical catapult	Understanding of technology	Throwing rubber – disruption
	'B for balloon'	Initial sound practice	Disturbing concentration of others
	Birds have stripes	Knowledge of natural world	Disturbing concentration of others
9.45	Discusses friend's eyes and choice of pencil	Accuracy and attention to detail	Disturbing concentration of others
9.46	Stands up and colours at table	Comfortable working position	Disturbing concentration of others
9.50	Describes picture	Expression about relationships	Disturbing concentration of others

interrupted and therefore learning undermined. However, Ros *also* values talk and interaction between children both as a medium of learning and as a necessary means of sustaining and developing a positive social climate in her classroom. Set against these criteria, the child's self-talk, interaction with others and movement around the room could be considered legitimate, worthwhile activity, or at least not self-evidently problematic, as her 'stressed' interpretations would have construed it. Just how sustained does engagement have to be in order to conform to her criteria of good learning? After all, for adults as well as for children, 'loafing about, doodling, gazing out of the window and chatting . . . are necessary breaks from more effortful, deliberate forms of learning, and are often the outward face of learning strategies that are valuable in their own right' (Claxton 1990: 157).

Setting an alternative interpretation alongside the original reading helped Ros to free her thinking from attachment to a particular meaning. By becoming aware of and questioning the values implicit in her interpretations, she was able to refine and rethink her expectations. Through these observations, she reminded herself of other norms and values which were also important to her and which, applied to Jamie's behaviour, would enable it to be viewed in a more positive light. By setting an alternative reading of the child's behaviour, consistent with her professional values, alongside the more negative reading, she was able to bring about a qualitative shift in her perception of Jamie and his response to her teaching, which in turn affected her behaviour towards him. She was also able to ask questions about the expectations implicit in her negative interpretations, and consider how these might need to be readjusted.

As Ros's experience illustrates, the sense that we ascribe to classroom events depends not only upon the personal resources that we have available (e.g. our previous knowledge, experience, values, beliefs), but also upon what we happen to *select* from our personal resources to use on a particular occasion. This selection is, in turn, affected by many personal, interpersonal and external factors including our emotional state, school climate, the expectations of colleagues and parents, and the history of our relationships with particular classes and individuals.

Recognising the norms inherent in judgements

In my own in-service work, I tend to register concern if people close their eyes when listening to a lecture, say, or during a whole-group discussion or plenary session. My automatic reaction is to worry that this indicates a withdrawal of interest, participation or goodwill, or lack of sufficient stimulation and involvement in the activity. I have to make a conscious effort to consider alternative possibilities: perhaps the person is tired or unwell, or, more positively, perhaps closed eyes are an *aid to concentration*. Perhaps the person is taking some time out to think hard about a train of thought that has been stimulated by the discussion, and this is a sign of involvement and learning, not disengagement. People have different learning preferences. Though I myself find it hard to concentrate on a lecture if I cannot *see* the person, I know that others with an auditory preference may find the visual signals too distracting; closed eyes *may* therefore be just an indication of a different preferred learning style to my own and not a reason for anxiety and intervention.

In most of our thinking in everyday life, including thinking in classrooms, we are not consciously aware of the norms and values which are implicit in our judgements and which lead us to interpret behaviour, learning, progress and achievement in particular ways. In the example drawn from my own work with adult learners, my 'concern' arises because I am implicitly using the criteria of 'open eyes', 'alert expression' and 'active contribution' by participants as norms for evaluating the impact of my teaching. Once these criteria are made explicit, I can appreciate their limitations. Open eyes, alert expression and active contribution certainly are valid criteria, but not the *only* valid criteria for evaluating participants' interest, involvement and learning. Not all active contributions are necessarily indicative of positive involvement and learning. Conversely, people can also give every indication in their body language of interest and involvement, but actually be miles away.

Of course, it is possible, too, that a spontaneous reaction may actually be accurate; that a person closing his or her eyes actually *is* manifesting some sort of disengagement and that some action needs to be taken, on my part, either there and then, or in rethinking the situation after the event. A contrasting reading of the situation is not necessarily more accurate than an immediate interpretation. However, we can be more secure in using our judgements to guide subsequent action if we are aware of the many factors influencing judgements, and if we have considered alternatives and checked out the grounds upon which spontaneous judgements are based (Abercrombie 1989: 17).

The unreliability of obvious, common-sense interpretations can be illustrated by the experience of a secondary teacher, Nicky, who spent a day shadowing her tutor group. In one lesson, she was surprised and pleased to see a girl who was not known for her concentration apparently sustain rapt attention throughout the lesson. The teacher had spent much of the lesson addressing the whole class, and Nicky's impression was that the girl's eyes never left the teacher's face. Talking to the girl afterwards, though, she was puzzled that she did not seem to recall much of what the lesson had been about. She asked the girl why. 'Oh, I wasn't listening to what she *said*, Miss,' the girl replied. 'I was watching her lips. Don't you think she has interesting lips?'

Clearly we should not underestimate the potential for classroom events to surprise and outwit our spontaneous interpretations, even when the meaning strikes us as self-evident. This story illustrates that it may be necessary and fruitful to pursue alternative interpretations, even when our immediate impressions suggest that pupils' responses were entirely satisfactory. The process of contradicting can work in both directions. It can be used to challenge and rethink a concern about classroom learning; or it can be used to review and reconsider a judgement that worthwhile learning has occurred. Both can be important in fulfilling our responsibilities towards children.

Normative judgements and equality issues

It is particularly important to be aware of how implicit norms, expectations and values affect our evaluations of classroom events and children's learning when teachers are working with children whose cultural and linguistic backgrounds differ significantly from their own. The work of Shirley Brice Heath (1983) has been influential in drawing attention to cultural differences which affect children's learning and achievements in school. Through a careful analysis of home–school differences, she showed how children might come to be seen by their teachers as disruptive or uncooperative when they were in fact behaving in accordance with a different set of social norms. For instance, children who found it difficult to stop chipping in at story time were seen by their teachers as lacking in self-control, when in fact they were behaving in accordance with the cultural practices of their communities where reading stories was considered a social activity, and where participation and involvement were expressed through oral contributions to the unfolding of the story. Similarly, children who carried on doing whatever they were doing, rather than stopping when they were told, were acting in accordance with their own community's preference for allowing children to control the duration of their own activities. Becoming aware of such cultural differences offers a new perspective on behaviour that might otherwise cause us to begin to form a negative picture of children's willingness to conform to the rules of the classroom. It opens up the need to find ways to bridge those differences, either by expanding our own reper-toire of learning opportunities in the classroom or by finding ways of communicating with children about the rules that they will be expected to abide by in school.

This is just one example of how the norms that we operate with respect to how we recognise and celebrate quality, achievement or progress can lead us to overlook qualities of children's learning which fall outside those norms. Chris Searle (1995), ex-head teacher of a Sheffield comprehensive school, laments the narrow concept of 'achievement' which focuses on examination success with respect to a predetermined curriculum, and neglects the stunning multi-lingual achievements of students who every day successfully move between different languages and cultures, managing the wide-ranging linguistic demands at school and outside and supporting and interpreting on behalf of family members who as yet have only limited command of English. When we talk of under-achievement or less able children, what norms of achievement or ability are we making use of, and what other human qualities and evidence of achievements are we neglecting to consider? Which children benefit from the application of these norms, and which children do they disadvantage?

Different views of learning and achievement

One striking example of the very different qualities that will be perceived in the same piece of work, when different ways of thinking about learning are brought to bear, is provided by Michael Armstrong (1990). Concerned about the impoverished view of children's writing implicit in the original National Curriculum statements of attainment, he examines a piece of work, 'When I was Naughty' (see Figure 4.1). This was chosen as an example of Level 2 features of writing by the National Curriculum English Working Group, who described it as follows.

Figure 4.1 'When I was naughty'

This is a simple chronological account with a clear story structure, including a conventional beginning, narrative middle and end. The sentences are almost all demarcated, though via the graphic, comic strip layout and not via capital letters and punctuation. The spelling is almost entirely meaningful and recognisable. In several cases it shows that the author has correctly grasped the patterns involved, even though the individual spellings are wrong (e.g. trooth, eny, owt, sumthing, cubad). The handwriting occasionally mixes upper and lower case letters, though only at the beginnings and ends of words, not at random (Appendix 6).

Armstrong contrasts this 'thin' description of a young child's narrative achievement with his own interpretation based on a very different way of thinking about children's writing. His detailed analysis is too long to reproduce here. However, his conclusions give a flavour of his overall approach:

'When I was naughty' allows us to glimpse a young child's thought in all its imaginative richness. The artistry of its six year old author is apparent in every aspect of her story. In her exploitation of narrative style, with its formulas, suspense, its various concealments and revelations, its open-ness to interpretation. In her acceptance of constraint and her turning of constraint into opportunity . . . In her critical judgement, so apparent in her choice of vocabulary. In her concern to express her own sense of life in the ordered medium of written and drawn narrative. In short, in her appropriation of form.   (Armstrong 1990: 15)

Armstrong recognises that his approach reflects a fundamentally different view of learning – and of teaching – from that reflected in the account provided by the working group. Armstrong sees genuine learning as a struggle with meaning, and teaching as a process of interpreting and supporting the child's intellectual enterprise. His radical critique of the criteria set by the English Working Group provides a challenging standpoint from which to re-examine the criteria implicit in our own judgements, when we differentiate between good and poor work, for example, and when we judge progress. It reminds us not to take those judgements for granted, even if they can be substantiated by evidence, but to think about the origins of the criteria that we use, and their consequences for our assessments of the learning and progress of particular children.

All these examples illustrate, in different ways, why it is important, in thinking through teaching, not to take our immediate interpretations at face value. The discipline of trying to search out a positive reading of the situation to set alongside a negative reading (and sometimes vice versa), helps to uncover the values and expectations that underlie our sense of dissatisfaction with some aspect of our teaching, or with children's responses to our teaching. Becoming aware of them means that we can re-examine them. In some cases this may mean that we no longer perceive the behaviour or learning as a problem. Alternatively, if we find that they do indeed stand up under scrutiny, we can think about what might be done to enable children to be more successful in realising our aspirations for their learning.

Contradicting and reframing

Further illustration of the potential for classroom events to lend themselves to more than one interpretation can be found in the literature relating to the technique of reframing (e.g. Molnar and Lindquist 1989). Reframing requires the teacher to come up with a positive alternative interpretation of problem behaviour and then to act in ways that are consistent with it. The theory is that by thinking and acting differently, the teacher will change the dynamics of the situation and so the behaviour itself will be affected.

For an educator, reframing means finding a new perceptual 'frame' for problem behaviour, one that is positive, fits the facts of the situation, and is plausible to the people involved. A reframing will also suggest how to act differently in the problem situation.   (Molnar and Lindquist 1989: 46)

Molnar and Lindquist provide a number of examples of reframing to illustrate what is involved. In one example, two boys (Bob and Pete) were consistently failing to follow rules about entering the classroom in the morning and getting straight down to work. Bob would stand at Pete's desk chatting and ignore the teacher's continual requests to sit down. It was creating a stressful start to each day and preventing the teacher from carrying out essential administrative tasks. The teacher decided to try reframing, and came up with a plausible, alternative interpretation as follows:

Original negative interpretation	*Reframed positive interpretation*
The two boys are trying to waste time, get out of doing their work and cause a rough time for me.	The two boys are good friends who want to spend time together first thing every morning as a way of affirming their bond of friendship.

The next step was to act consistently with this reframing. When Bob came in and stood at Pete's desk next morning, the teacher did not ask him to go to his desk, but commented on the importance of the boys' friendship. Not surprisingly, the boys did not at first take the teacher's comment seriously. When she made a similar comment the next day, though, their disbelief started to give way to surprise. Eventually, as the teacher persisted with this alternative strategy, the problem was resolved.

It is essential, for the success of reframing, that the new, positive interpretation should be plausible not just to the teacher but also to the students. Initially, as in this case, the pupils may be startled by the change in the teacher's response to their behaviour and assume that the teacher is being sarcastic. However, if the teacher persists in acting consistently with the reframed interpretation, and if this is also plausible to the students, significant changes in the dynamics of a problem situation can be brought about.

In a second case, a teacher was concerned about a young adolescent boy, Rick, who was physically much taller and more strongly built than any of his peers, and who was assuming an anti-authority position as a tough guy or rebel: 'Throughout the school year he tried to live up to his image by not completing assignments, not participating in regular classroom activities, distracting teachers and intimidating other students' (Molnar and Lindquist 1989: 53). The teacher described the various strategies he had tried to get through to Rick, ranging from sympathetic negotiation to confrontation. None had brought any success. He then went on to explain how he had used reframing to help turn things around, when the class were involved in preparing a performance for the school and parents. Rick's attitude was having a negative effect on the other students, and the teacher felt that he urgently needed to do something that would have a positive effect.

During a rehearsal in which the students were practising hand movements to a song and Rick was acting silly, I walked over to him and told him that I could appreciate his discomfort in participating. As an adult about his size, I, too, felt awkward in trying to do the activities. I invited him to feel free to step aside and just watch, as I was doing.

Rick seemed a bit taken aback. He did not participate for the rest of that period, but he also did not create any disruption. During our next rehearsal, I was surprised to see Rick make some serious attempts to join in with the rest of the class, and as the practice sessions continued, Rick's involvement became more serious.

In order to reframe Rick's behaviour, the teacher needed to set aside his previous perception of Rick as rebellious and anti-authority, and find a new, non-negative interpretation that was plausible both to himself and to Rick. To do so can be difficult, not just because the perception has been reinforced over many months, but also because teachers may be under considerable peer pressure not to change their behaviour in ways that colleagues might regard as giving in or lowering standards. Nevertheless, the teacher was impressed with the long-term effects of his reframing. Over the weeks following this reframing, there was a noticeable improvement in Rick's participation and attitude.

Contradicting and reframing

These examples of reframing may be helpful in illustrating how the same situation can lend itself to contrasting interpretations, as well as showing how particular interpretations themselves form part of the ongoing dynamics of the situation. There are some differences, however, between contradicting and reframing that are worth noting. Unlike reframing, contradicting is not a technique which can be used on its own as a means of addressing a concern. It is one of a set of interpretive strategies which operate *together* to explore the meaning of classroom events and generate new possibilities for the development of practice. As well as challenging an initial reading of the situation ('Costas didn't listen to the instructions', 'Asad didn't understand the main points of the lesson'), contradicting can be used at any point in the reflective process to challenge the norms and assumptions implicit in possibilities being considered.

Moreover, with contradicting, the search for contrasting interpretations can work in both directions. We search for positive interpretations that question whether what we initially perceived as a problem actually *is* a matter for concern; or conversely, we can look for negative interpretations that suggest it may be necessary to look more closely at what we initially perceived to be a perfectly satisfactory state of affairs. The shift in both directions can operate in the interests of children. In the first case, we may avoid changing a situation that does not need changing; in the second, we are alerted to an area where we may be able to make some constructive intervention that would not otherwise have come to our attention.

The complementary nature of the different moves

The two questioning moves that we have examined so far complement one another because they each focus on a feature of the situation that the other takes for granted. Making connections accepts the particular perception of the situation as something to be concerned about, or thought more about, and focuses on possible connections with the learning environment. Contradicting focuses on the thinking itself that led us to identify something as a matter for concern, and encourages us to reconsider the grounds for interpreting it in this way. Each raises important, yet different questions from the other; used together they can provide a richer, more complex understanding of classroom events, and open up a wider range of possible ways of responding, than either could generate alone.

Although the contradicting move emphasises the importance of being prepared to question the norms and assumptions that are operating implicitly in our judgements and evaluations of classroom teaching, this is not to imply that our everyday thinking is somehow defective. Our expectations and values are part of the necessary equipment that enable us to make sense of children's responses and evaluate our own contribution to their development. We need our norms of good learning to alert us to issues requiring further thought, to concerns that we need to pursue and may need to take action about. The facility to uncover them and make them explicit rather than simply trust our intuitive judgement is part of our professional responsibility in keeping our own thinking under review; it is also an important source of power, helping both to generate and check out new ideas that emerge for enhancing children's learning.

CHAPTER 5
Taking a child's eye view

This move involves trying to step outside our teacher's (adult's) frames of reference and *appreciate the meaning and logic* underlying what children say and do *from their point of view.* We ask ourselves: 'What does this mean/feel like for the child?'

So far, in examining the individual questioning moves, discussion has remained within a teacher – or adult – frame of reference. We have been looking through the teacher's eyes, exploring the different interpretations that can be generated to help understand a situation from the teacher's point of view. The third questioning move, taking a child's eye view, involves making a conscious effort to shift outside our own frames of reference and look at the situation afresh from the learners' perspective.

This move reflects an appreciation that children are active meaning-makers in their own right. They, too, are continually making sense of classroom situations, and their meanings play just as important a part as our own in the unfolding dynamics of classroom interaction. As active agents, children have their own agendas which they pursue at least as vigorously as those that teachers attempt to negotiate with them. For instance, when we were probing Asad's perceived failure to understand the main points of the lesson (Chapter 2), one possibility considered was that Asad had something else pressing on his mind, and that his teachers' preoccupation with the Spanish Armada did not happen to figure highly in his order of priorities. It is unlikely that we can gain an adequate understanding of a situation simply by focusing on features of the child's response in relation to our agenda. We have to consider what the child's own agenda might be and how their learning and behaviour might make sense in *their* terms.

In the dynamics of classroom interaction, it is likely too that children will be seeking to exercise influence and control over *our* agenda. Teachers who have discussed the incident between Emer and Costas (Chapter 1), before hearing Emer's own reconstruction, have raised the possibility that Costas *had* listened to and understood perfectly well the teacher's instruction, but *chose* not to follow it because he hoped to persuade her to let him play the game (as well as, or instead of, merely putting it away). Costas was perhaps trying to gain himself the opportunity of playing his favourite game, even though he knew it was not part of his teacher's agenda. Both this and Emer's interpretation provide interesting new perspectives on Costas's originally perceived failure to listen to the instructions, achieved predominantly by attempting to reread what occurred from the child's point of view.

In this chapter, I examine the important, complementary role that taking a child's eye view has to play in the process of thinking through teaching. I use a number of examples drawn from the Enfield teachers' work, and from the literature, to explore the kinds of insights that can be gained through this means into children's intellectual and cognitive understandings, and into their emotional and social worlds. I look at the part that children's own accounts of their experience can play in helping us to see things through their eyes, and consider the important complementary role that our everyday observations have to play in enabling us to understand the dynamics of classroom learning from the learners' point of view.

Bridging the inevitable gap between learners and teachers

There is a well-known passage in Laurie Lee's *Cider With Rosie*, where Laurie is told by the teacher, on his first day at school, to 'sit there for the present'. Laurie obediently sits and waits for the promised present and, when it fails to materialise, vows that he 'aint going back there again'. The story is a poignant reminder of the inescapable gap that exists between children's meanings and those of their teachers, as Donaldson notes (1978: 17). The meanings that children construct, the sense that they make of class-room life, and of the teacher's efforts to enable and assist their learning, will inevitably be different from those of their teachers because of the different knowledge and experience that they draw upon in making their interpretations.

Many teachers do try to put themselves in the child's shoes, and see how that helps to understand children's reactions to their experience at school. However, it is hard to remember, once the world has been organised in terms of our adult concepts and categories, what it was like to be confronted by the task of making sense of it all. This was brought home to one teacher, Sue, when sharing a book with Anna, age six, who was just beginning to pay careful attention to the print on the page. Anna suddenly pointed to a word she had seen before, in other books. Turning to Sue, her eyes shining with excitement, she announced triumphantly her realisation that a word looks the same each time it appears, even in different books!

Her excited discovery reminded Sue that until you *know* how the print system works, it is perfectly possible that a word might look different (be spelt differently?) when it appears in different contexts. It is just as possible, for a child learning to make sense of the world, that the print system might operate according to *other* principles already familiar to children. For example, children know that objects with the same label (chairs, houses, cars, teddy bears) do not look all the same. They may even also know already that letters do not always look the same every time you see them (different fonts, sizes and styles of handwriting, upper and lower case letters). So it is at least plausible that *words* might not look the same each time you meet them, until you have had enough experience to recognise the patterns.

Sue's story reveals Anna as an active learner, generating her own hypotheses about how print works, and checking these out against her own experience and in interaction with her teacher. It reminds us of the complexity of the work children do in making sense of the world, and the sophistication of the thinking required gradually to bring it all under control. Taking a child's eye view helps us to recognise more fully children's accomplishments and to cross the inevitable gap between teachers' ways of thinking and those of children in order to support their efforts to learn.

New awareness of difficulties

Shifting into the child's perspective can also help us to gain a new appreciation of the difficulties that an apparently simple task or instruction can present to a child, as well as the intelligent effort reflected in the child's response. For example, Deb (one of the Enfield teachers) was doing some dance work in PE with the whole class. During the warm-up session, the children were moving around on the floor. Then Deb gave the instruction 'Stop and sit up!' One child (fairly new to English) stopped and *stood* up. Deb's immediate response was to correct him, and repeat the instruction. She describes what happened next as follows:

> He sort of bent his knees and hovered looking at me, quite clearly not sure what he should be doing. I was just beginning to get exasperated because the rest of the class were waiting, when I suddenly saw in his face all uncertainty and doubt about what I meant. 'What does she mean sit up? Up means "stand", doesn't it? I know "sit down", but I was already down and she said "up", so I got up.'

In the midst of this interaction, Deb suddenly saw a logic behind the child's response. It is logical to assume – if you are already sitting down – that an instruction containing 'up' will be to *stand* up. She realised that the child's response was borne not of confusion about language use per se, but of his particular *grasp* of the situation which led him to expect the instruction to require a particular course of action. The subtleties and complexities governing the use of 'simple' instructions such as 'sit up', 'sit down', and 'stand up' were further underlined by what followed.

> So I said, 'Look at the others. What are they doing?' He said 'Sitting'. So I said, 'Right, you sit down'.

As Deb gave the instruction, she registered (with some dismay) that what she was now telling the child to do was actually different from her original instruction. Now, the right thing to do, apparently, was to sit *down*. What sense was the child supposed to make of this verbal shift? Would he have finished up more confused than ever? Reflecting on this incident after the event, Deb recognised that, on the positive side, the child's response showed that he was not just relying on following the others, but actually listening to and trying to make sense of her language. The incident served to heighten both her awareness of the complexities confronting learners new to English that are inherent in such everyday linguistic routines, and her appreciation of the child's effort and accomplishments.

Giving the child reason

The example illustrates what Donald Schon calls 'giving the child reason', a process which, he argues, is at the heart of reflective practice (Schon 1988). Giving the child reason means that we start out from an assumption that the child's response makes sense, if we can only penetrate that sense and appreciate where the child is coming from. Illustrating this, Schon discusses a series of exchanges between a teacher and a child – carried out over several days – about 'where the sun is'. At first, the teacher thinks that the child does not realise that the sun is there, in the sky, even on a day when it can't be seen through the clouds. The teacher continues to ask questions, trying to reason with the child and to demonstrate that the sun can still be there even when it is not visible. Gradually, though, she starts to wonder if perhaps the child is interpreting the idea of 'where the sun is' more literally than she, using 'where' to mean the actual location of the sun in the sky. She works out a way of questioning the child so that she is able to confirm this possibility.

Clearly, we should take care not to assume that any gap between teachers' understandings and those of pupils is necessarily a consequence of the inevitable greater knowledge and experience of adults in comparison with children. Here, the misunderstanding may have come about because the child, George, did not imagine that the teacher could possibly think he did not know that the sun was in the sky. Therefore, he interpreted her question 'Where is the sun today?' (on a cloudy day) as a request for a precise location. He answered 'I don't know' because he couldn't actually *see* where the sun was. The teacher, on the other hand, certainly did think it was possible (though unexpected and puzzling) that George was confused, and had not noticed the confusing ambiguity implicit in her own question.

The reason behind 'wrong' answers

It is particularly important to try to penetrate the logic of learners' responses when the immediate temptation is to construe them as evidence of confusion or misunderstanding. If we make the effort to search out the logic, when it is not immediately obvious, we can gain a valuable new perspective on the intelligent thought that lies behind a wrong or puzzling response. For example, Will Swann (1987) describes what went through his mind as he observed and talked to five-year-old Tanya as she was drawing round some shapes. He asked her how many sides the shape had, and in response she took three other squares from the box and laid them out in a line with the sides touching. He put the squares away and asked her to show him a side. The child pointed to the centre of the top surface of one square. His initial reaction was to assume that she did not understand the word 'side', but he was not satisfied with this conclusion.

> Although her responses appear to be random guesses, they may not have been. Tanya will have met the word 'side' many times out of school in expressions such as 'put it to one side', 'which side are you on?', 'side by side' and 'the side of the cupboard'. In the exchange recounted, 'side' takes on another, less familiar meaning. Tanya's responses make sense if we treat her as an active interpreter of my

questions. Her first response was to put some squares *side by side;* her second response was consistent with interpreting a side as a plane surface of an object, as in the 'side of the cupboard'. Tanya will have made sense of my question in terms of her existing knowledge. I suspect her 'difficulty' was largely illusory, and is more accurately described as a communication failure, but on whose part?

(Swann 1988: 92)

Even when answers are unambiguously wrong, as in addition or subtraction, it is important for the teacher to try to penetrate the logic of the child's thinking that led to the wrong answer in order to be able to provide help that actually connects to the child's existing understandings. Patrick Easen (1995) noticed, for example, that the child who did the sums in Figure 5.1 had a systematic procedure for carrying out the calculation, even though it led (systematically) to wrong answers.

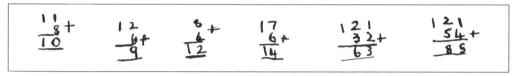

Figure 5.1 A child's procedure for addition

Easen offers a number of detailed observations of children engaging in mathematical thinking, providing further illustration of his theory that 'if you look enough and dig deep enough there are often some unsuspected strengths that the child possesses' (Easen 1987: 36).

In another fascinating study, this time of children's mistakes in oral reading, Bettelheim and Zelan (1991) argue that we should take care not to assume that errors are simply a reflection of inattention, inexperience or lack of knowledge on the part of the child. Rather, they may be indicative of thoughts and feelings aroused in the child by the text and by the activity of reading to the teacher.

For just as we tend to see what we want to see and often distort or fail to see what we do not wish to see, maybe children make mistakes in reading (which depends so much on seeing) because they want to see a different word on the page than the one printed there. So an error in reading could be due to a desire to read differently, not to an inability to read correctly.   (Bettelheim and Zelan 1991: 95)

They suggest that we need to think about how specific misreadings connect to the child's personal experience, interests and priorities, and try to respond to them in such a way that the child realises that these thoughts and feelings are being acknowledged and taken seriously by the teacher. When they tried to respond in this way, Bettelheim and Zelan found that children would often spontaneously correct their errors without any further prompting.

Enabling learning

Shifting from the teacher's frame of reference into that of the learner may also be essential in order for the teacher to understand learners' questions and provide appropriate help. A secondary teacher, for example, describes an interaction with 15-year-old Diane during a science lesson on gravitational pull (Henderson 1996). As the teacher finished his explanation, Diane asked a question which made it evident that she had not understood; he tried to answer her question by providing further examples, but she was clearly still confused. The teacher continues the story as follows:

I realised that I didn't understand her question any more than she understood my answer. I had been working from, thinking with, the perspective of a spectator out in space, measuring the distances in the picture in my mind. That was the whole that I was assuming, working to lead my students to that same end. I wanted them to hold that image, watching the worlds turn from that neutral and removed point of view. Instead, I felt that image crumble. Diane was seeing the problem from a radically different perspective, but I had no idea what it was. I needed to see the problem from her point of view, and so I went looking for some parts from which we could reconstruct a new whole.
'Can you ask your question again?' I asked her.
'Okay,' she said. 'What I want to know is, would it be different if you were standing there?'
'On the planet?'
'Yes, yes, on Venus.'
   In a flash, I understood – not only her question, but, more importantly the perspective from which her question came. I had been watching the solar system from a remote perspective, thinking of gravitation in the more abstract sense as the force that binds planets to stars. She had imagined gravitation in the more immediate and personal sense, as that which holds us to the earth. What effects could she feel, could she experience, as a consequence of greater or weaker gravitational forces from the sun? How did my abstract lesson, the mathematics of which she understood, have meaning in her context?
   By drawing on our mass media experience of watching astronauts apparently weightless in orbit, I was able to help her to see the answer to her question. I'll spare the reader the rest of the scientific details. The point is that I was able to visit with her in her perspective. More importantly, I was able to help her to move to a new and larger view point. This time I knew she was there with me.

(Henderson 1996: 116–17)

Visiting with learners in *their* perspective may be essential not just for answering questions but for planning what the next steps might be for particular individuals' learning. This issue was brought to my attention, in my own research into children's writing development, when Adrian, one of the two children I was studying, started writing what he termed an 'adventure story' entirely in dialogue. While giving every encouragement to his efforts, his teachers and I were convinced that he needed to learn how to embed the dialogue in some more narrative detail, in order to carry the reader along. Yet in spite of his teachers' continual attempts to encourage and assist him in this direction, Adrian steadfastly resisted their efforts, claiming again and again that no-one understood what he was trying to do with his writing.

It was only some time later, when I was re-examining the overall pattern of his development over the year, that it occurred to me that there might be other ways of interpreting Adrian's use of dialogue where it would indeed not have been an appropriate next step to add more narrative detail. Suppose that what he had in mind (though did not make explicit) was a comic-book format, in which all the narrative detail was contained in the surrounding pictures? Or (as I eventually concluded) that what he was actually engaged in was writing an adventure-story script for television, based on the vivid repartee and action that he constructed in his mind, where pure dialogue would be all that, at this stage, was required? If our efforts to support and facilitate children's learning are to be successful then they need to be congruent with learners' own purposes, with the way that they construe their needs as learners, as reflected in the difficulties they encounter and the kinds of help that they seek, and their responses to our efforts to help.

This, and the other examples examined so far, illustrate the different perspectives upon pupils' thinking and learning, and any difficulties that they appear to be experiencing, that can be opened up when we try to take a child's eye view. When children behave in ways which surprise or puzzle us, when they offer apparently irrelevant contributions to discussion, when they fail to do what we ask, or do not interpret tasks as we intend, it may be only by shifting out of our own frame of reference that we become able to appreciate the intelligent thinking that lies behind their response. When we make a conscious effort to make sense of classroom events from the learners' point of view, we are able to see the situation with fresh eyes and notice things that might otherwise escape our notice.

Emotional and social dimensions of school experience

Moreover, it is not just children's developing thinking and understanding that we need to try to identify, but also their emotional and social worlds. We cannot understand their responses to our teaching, and other aspects of school life, without paying attention to, and seeking to penetrate with equal effort, the social and emotional dimensions of their experience. Doing so can help to appreciate more fully, and see ways of supporting, other areas of their development. It can help to gain a new perspective on aspects of pupils' behaviour which we find worrying or puzzling in some way; to reach a better understanding of why some resist our best efforts to teach them; and to find ways of bringing back in those who have become marginalised or excluded.

A moving account of teachers' efforts to understand and appreciate one child's emotional growth is provided by Mary Jane Drummond in her book *Assessing Children's Learning* (Drummond 1993: 44). She describes a long drawn-out leave-taking ritual which one boy, James, and his mother had developed, by the start of his third year in school, as a way of avoiding distress on separation at the start of each school day.

The route they took to school led down a narrow road through some trees to a spot where the school drive branched off the right, leading uphill again to the school front door, about 50 yards away. James and his mother stopped at this spot and kissed each other good-bye. James bolted up the drive to the front door, while his mother waited on the same spot. From the doorstep of the school, James waved and blew kisses, which were warmly returned. His mother then started walking up hill, and as soon as she walked away, James came into school and flew down the corridor to his classroom. He stood on the classroom windowsill (luckily a low one) and waited until he could see his mother coming back into sight through the trees, as she walked homewards up the hill behind the school. When she saw him at the window, a second round of waves and kisses ensued, and then, satisfied, James was ready to join the class.   (Drummond 1993: 44)

Mary Jane (who was the head teacher at the school) explains that his teachers had accepted this ritual as a necessary, but not very desirable, compromise. 'We were none of us convinced that it was the best way to help James to learn to part more easily from his mother' (p. 46). However, one morning, James's teacher was unavoidably delayed, and Mary Jane was supervising the class until her arrival. James chose to work on a table where she had set out some drawing materials, and produced a drawing using white chalk and charcoal on grey paper. Mary Jane was impressed at the way the drawing 'was evocative of the damp, moist mist that was curling around the trees outside the classroom window'. Asking the title of the picture, James told her it was 'Waving Good-bye to my Mother'.

As a result of looking closely at this picture and discussing it with colleagues, the teachers were led to revise their judgements about the leave-taking and its relationship to James's emotional development. They achieved this by trying to think themselves into the child's emotional world, interpreting the picture from that point of view.

James had drawn himself from the outside, from the other side of the classroom window, looking in through the mist and condensation. He had drawn what his mother saw, as she waved good bye to him for the last time that morning. But he has also drawn an emotional portrait of himself – as a child who is both distressed and courageous, a child who hates parting but who has learned to say good bye, a child who is near to tears but remains serene and composed – a very realistic self-portrait. And the picture seems to represent not just this self, but James's aware-ness of the characteristics of this self, as something to be proud of.
                    (Drummond 1993: 46)

This interpretation enabled them to gain a new perspective upon – and appreciation of – the extent of James's emotional development. He was not yet seven years old, yet he understood and was able to represent his own, mixed feelings about parting from his mother. Moreover, as Mary Jane points out, 'he had learnt to represent them not only from his own point of view but from his mother's' (p. 46).

The example illustrates yet again how taking the child's eye view can help us to trans-form an existing, somewhat negatively tinged *adult* perspective on aspects of a child's behaviour – this time in the emotional domain – into a new appreciation of the sophistication of the child's understandings and achievements. It can help to ensure that we do not underestimate the knowledge and understanding reflected in their responses, because these do not appear to conform to our teacher/adult expectations.

Fear and the development of coping strategies

Exploring the emotional dimensions of school learning can lead to a deeper under-standing of the many pressures and anxieties that pupils experience and which may lead them to develop defensive strategies that directly impede their learning. John Holt, for example, confesses to the surprise and shock which he experienced when children told him that fear was a central driving force guiding their responses to school learning: 'They said they were afraid of failing, afraid of being kept back, afraid of being called stupid, afraid of feeling themselves stupid' (Holt 1990: 71).

The children's comments drew attention to the vital difference between what teach-ers intend and what pupils actually experience. Just because we *intend* to create learning environments which welcome and value all children, we cannot assume that this is indeed how they are experienced by children. From his conversations with children, Holt concluded: 'Even in the kindest and gentlest of schools, children are afraid, many of them a great deal of the time, some of them almost all the time. This is a hard fact of life to deal with' (p. 71).

Once he realised that children's classroom responses needed to be read, first and foremost, in terms of fear, he began to recognise the strategies he observed as ways of coping with these feelings: helping them to get through the day unscathed. For example, he tells the story of Ruth who had perfected a highly effective strategy which involved getting the teacher to do the work for her. Holt describes a session with her which 'opened his eyes':

> It was slow work. Question after question met only silence. She did nothing, said nothing, just sat and looked at me through those glasses, and waited. Each time, I had to think of a question easier and more pointed than the last, until I finally found one so easy that she would feel safe in answering it. So we inched our way along until suddenly, looking at her as I waited for an answer to a question, I saw with a start that she was not at all puzzled by what I had asked her. In fact, she was not even thinking about it. She was coolly appraising me, weighing my patience, waiting for that next, sure-to-be-easier question. I thought 'I've been had!'.
>
> (Holt 1990: 39)

Although some of the coping strategies, as in this case, had the effect of directly impeding learning, others were more enabling. In fact, it is unrealistic to imagine that learners can be set free from fear, Holt observes, because there are always tensions associ-ated with learning. In some cases, the strategies pupils used – though initially puzzling to the teacher – were eventually recognised as ways of coping with these inevitable tensions.

Many other educators and researchers have also used the notion of coping strategies to explore and explain pupils' responses to school learning (e.g. Hargreaves 1972;

Pollard 1985; Woods 1980). Guy Claxton (1990) emphasises the positive function of defensive strategies. 'Sometimes,' he argues, 'it makes better sense to decline the learning invitation and instead to escape from, avoid or in other ways defend against the situation'. Learning is not always the most intelligent response. He provides an analysis of some defensive strategies 'used in both classroom and staffroom' (see Figure 5.2) which teachers may find helpful in reflecting upon pupils' characteristic responses to classroom activities. If we look upon these responses, from the pupils' point of view, as strategies chosen for good reason in order to cope with the demands of the situation, we will more readily recognise the potential for change. It may be possible to identify ways in which we might be instrumental in encouraging pupils to choose more learning-oriented responses.

- **Leaving:** physically removing yourself from source of threat or stress (truancy, going sick)
- **Hiding:** endeavouring to make oneself invisible so that threatening situations are minimised
- **Tensing:** suppressing bad feeling by preventing parts of body from quivering
- **Denying:** becoming tactically unconscious of what is going on around you
- **Dulling:** using drugs to replace bad feelings with good, and tension with relaxation
- **Depressing:** becoming tactically unconscious of what is going on inside you, particularly bad feelings
- **Distracting:** filling up the space left by tensing, denying or depressing with safer activity (e.g. TV watching, dreaming)
- **Regressing:** not having to try by denying capability
- **Blaming:** not having to try by virtue of denying responsibility
- **Displacing:** righteous indignation or hostility redirected towards 'safer' others (e.g. taking it out on cat)
- **Denigrating:** another variant of blaming – attacking learning event and person responsible for it
- **Rationalising:** telling hardluck stories to gain sympathy and exoneration from responsibility
- **Exaggeration:** inflating the awfulness of events in order to convince self that no one could have coped
- **Compensating:** spending time doing the things you can do well, so that there is no time left for things you are afraid you will do badly
- **Specialising:** forming a group of people who are special, not understood by others and so not vulnerable to their criticism

---

Figure 5.2 Defending strategies (based on Claxton 1990)

Phillida Salmon (1995) stresses that pupils' willingness and ability to take up invitations to learn also depends upon the 'tact and delicacy' of the teacher in facilitating the learning process. Her notion of 'sociality', drawn from the work of Kelly (1955), offers another interpretation of what is meant here by taking the child's eye view, i.e. 'a broad and sensitive attention to how another construes the world' (Salmon 1995: 36). She acknowledges, however, that it is much easier for teachers to enter imaginatively the lives of children whose childhoods seem comparable to their own:

But for other young people, whose out-of-school lives are more mysterious, their identities less accessible to us, the message we offer may be less confident, less clear. Only by working to enlarge these limits of sociality is it possible to extend more widely the invitation which teaching essentially entails.   (Salmon 1995: 38)

Group membership and the construction of identity

One important resource available for teachers seeking to deepen their understanding of pupils' experiences in and out of school is a growing tradition of research exploring the part that class, gender and race identities play in the choices made and strategies adopted by particular pupil groups (e.g. Willis 1977; Davies 1984; Mac An Ghaill 1988; 1994; Gillborn 1990; Mirza 1992). Careful not to generalise and imply that members of a particular group respond in the same way to particular features of school experience, researchers have been concerned with exploring how the diverse responses of individuals were shaped by their sense of their own class, gender and ethnic identities and how these identities, in turn, were shaped by features of school experience.

In a recent study, for example, Connolly (1998) provides a fascinating insight into the gendered and racialised worlds of young children in an infant school. He explores how children use discourses of race and gender to gain status, develop their sense of self and make sense of their experiences. Connolly argues that it is important for teachers to understand these processes – and in particular how peer relations affect children's responses to school experience – in order to assess their own practices and social relations in the school more generally.

One particularly interesting example discussed is the development, over a number of years, of a 'footballing' elite, whose games dominated the main part of the playground in morning break and at lunch times. This had been encouraged by the head teacher and another member of staff, both football enthusiasts, in part as a means of 'reaching out and engaging with a number of older (predominantly Black) boys perceived to be becoming disaffected with the school' (Connolly 1998: 86). Indeed, three-quarters of the footballing elite were Black, compared to one-quarter Black pupils within the school population as a whole.

Connolly analyses how the encouragement of this elite, intended in part as a multicultural, anti-racist strategy, unwittingly increased the likelihood of South Asian boys being either socially excluded and/or racially abused.

Football, more than many other group activities, was not only an inherently public affair but also a highly competitive one. It could be argued that games of football among the boys therefore provided one of the predominant social arenas in which masculine identities were lost and won. Within this context . . . not only were South Asian boys almost systematically excluded from football but, for those few who were able to play, they were more likely to be at the receiving end of racial abuse.

(Connolly 1998: 134)

In order to explain how this well-intentioned strategy brought about these effects, Connolly uses a sophisticated analysis of the interaction between race and gender discourses as they were used by the children to gain status, to establish their own identities, to explain and justify patterns of inclusion and exclusion, and interpret their own and others' behaviour. Such a sophisticated understanding of the complex relationship between race and gender relations is needed, Connolly argues, when schools embark on particular multicultural/anti-racist strategies. We need to look beyond our intentions and aspirations in order to examine the actual effects of our interventions upon the dynamics of inclusion and exclusion, as experienced by particular groups and individuals concerned.

The point is reiterated by other educators and researchers who have attempted to probe young people's reactions to efforts on the part of their teachers to acknowledge and build on diverse cultural backgrounds and experiences as part of curriculum activities. Kiddle (1999: 45), for example, notes the impact upon traveller children of teachers' well-intentioned efforts to value and give formal curriculum recognition to their distinctive experiences and life-styles.

> I expect most teachers of Travellers have heard the frustration and resignation in the tones of voice from children travelling with circuses when they report that they have been expected to give yet another talk about their way of life to their new classmates of that particular week. One child from a circus family tells me that now every time he goes into a new school he brings up the topic with the class teacher as soon as he can. He knows that at some stage during the stay he will be asked to give the talk, so now he offers to do it straight away at the beginning of the week so that he can 'get it over with' and then join the rest of the class.

The teachers involved would no doubt be taken aback to learn that such a strategy was experienced as unhelpful and unwelcome by this particular child. Indeed, it is a fine line that teachers have to tread between valuing diversity of experience on the one hand, and avoiding creating a sense of otherness and difference on the other. The point is not that we *ought to* be able to get it right every time; but that we must be constantly aware of the risk of getting it wrong, for particular individuals or for groups of children more generally. There can be no simple recipes or generalisations about what will be helpful and appropriate for every child.

Means of gaining access to children's perspectives

Talking to children is one way that we can gain insight into pupils' experiences and perspectives, and check out the impact of well-intentioned strategies. It has to be acknowledged, though, that the power differential operating in teacher–pupil relationships may well make it difficult for pupils to reveal to teachers what they really think and feel, especially if this is likely to be received as critical by the teachers concerned. That is why research has such an important part to play in expanding the resources we have available for trying to penetrate pupils' subjective experience and evaluate their responses to our teaching through their eyes. Kiddle's study of traveller children, subtitled 'A *voice for themselves*', is part of a burgeoning tradition of research which aims to give the views and experiences of children an opportunity to be heard; to set them alongside those of professionals and other adults, as a resource for reflecting upon and in some cases challenging the perspectives of those who claim to know their needs and to act in their interests.

A more powerful strategy than simply talking to children may be to involve them actively in an ongoing process of inquiry about how learning can be improved. Morwenna Griffiths and Carol Davies (1995) present a fascinating account of how they attempted to involve a succession of primary children in working out ways to enhance their experience of learning, particularly with respect to equal opportunities to learn (fairness) in the classroom. The children helped to identify the issues to be explored; they also helped to draw up questionnaires to assist classmates in expressing their views on particular topics and in monitoring their own progress towards goals that they had set for themselves. These teachers argue that junior age children are by no means too young to be reflecting on learning processes and study skills; that, if children's trust can be won and their experience genuinely tapped, such approaches can provide a powerful resource for learning for both teachers and children.

Close observation and listening can also be important means of making the imaginative shift involved in taking a child's eye view. Although it is important for learners to be consulted about their experience, for teachers not to assume that they can judge pupils' states of mind from observation alone, at the same time we cannot always be plying learners with questions about what they are thinking and feeling, about their motives, purposes and agendas. We must inevitably work much of the time from what we notice and hear in our everyday work with children, rather than by soliciting their views in a direct way.

The development of 'schema' theory

The power of observation as a means of understanding children's learning from the learner's perspective is well illustrated by some influential recent research in the area of early years education. Schema theory has been developed as the result of careful, sustained observation of young children's patterns of activity in early years classrooms (e.g. Athey 1990; Nutbrown 1999; Easen *et al.* 1992). In Athey's pioneering study, teachers, researchers and parents worked together to try to penetrate the thinking that lay behind recurrent patterns in children's play, behind the things that children paid attention to, and the remarks that they made, in the course of various activities. They gradually began to formulate their developing understanding in terms of particular schemas representing the predominant cognitive concerns that were directing children's choices of activity. Instead of looking for patterns in the *content* of the activities that children engaged in, they discovered continuities in the *forms of thought* that made sense of what otherwise might have appeared to be a series of quite disconnected activities.

Nutbrown (1999), for example, illustrates the 'threads of thinking' that might exist between four, apparently different activities, engaged in by a three-year-old over a period of six minutes.

First, he digs in the sand; then he moves on to make a cup from some clay; then he goes outside to 'hide' under the branches of a willow tree; next he paints – two ovals on a large sheet of paper with a dab in the centre of each. 'mices in cages,' he says . . . Considered in terms of *continuity of thought* he creates: a *hole* (in the sand), and a *container* (in the clay), he *hides* in an enveloping space (under the willow tree) and he represents two mice *enclosed in cages* (*using paint*). Reflected upon in this way, the links or *continuities* in his behaviour become apparent and can be described as part of his enveloping/enclosing schema, his predominant cognitive concern.

(Nutbrown 1999: 33, original emphasis)

These new insights into the development of young children's thinking were achieved because those involved persistently searched for meaning and continuity by trying to put themselves in the child's position, assuming that there was a logic and purpose to be discovered, even if it was not immediately obvious from an adult perspective. Observing children's actions with schemas (rather than simply content) allows us, Nutbrown observes, to interpret children's approaches to learning differently.

Schema theory has given new understanding as to why some children seem to become obsessed with one particular activity, repeating it over and over again. It has also helped to give new meaning and continuity to activity which, from an adult's perspective, seems to involve aimless 'flitting' from one activity to the next. It has offered not simply a new means of penetrating children's thinking but also a new way of conceptualising what is involved for teachers in feeding and nourishing children's scholastic interests:

It is through schemas, and the fitting of content to different schematic threads, that children's own constructions of reality can sometimes be identified and subsequent opportunities for further continuity in learning created. Looking at learning in this way can be a little like unlocking a door, shining a light on previously darkened areas, seeing anew.   (Nutbrown 1999: 33)

A complementary perspective

Although many of the examples explored in this chapter focus upon momentary interactions between teachers and children, the cumulative effect of such interactions upon children's sense of themselves, as people and as learners, should not be underestimated. Through our efforts to understand things from the pupils' perspective, we communicate caring for the learners and respect for their intelligence as competent individuals. Taking a child's eye view plays an important part in our repertoire of strategies for making sense of classroom events because, as one Enfield teacher said, it creates a dialogue in the teacher's mind in which the voice of the child is continually represented.

This third questioning move complements the two moves already discussed (making connections and contradicting) in a number of ways. It provides a set of additional standpoints from which to review and reflect on what happens in classrooms; it enables us to make new connections with the learning environment that might not otherwise have been visible; and also to challenge existing interpretations and judgements by suggesting contrasting readings of the situation that might not otherwise have come to mind.

Because taking a child's eye view also involves making connections and contradicting, there is inevitably an overlap between the various moves. Yet it is important, too, to maintain a distinction. Shifting into a frame of reference that is genuinely different from our own requires considerable effort; as this chapter illustrates, it is an effort that is vitally important in order to safeguard children's interests and ensure that teaching really does connect up with and build upon children's existing knowledge and understanding. Hence I have chosen to represent these three approaches to reflective analysis as three distinct moves, even though in practice they probably operate most effectively and powerfully when used fluidly and flexibly together rather than in any step-by-step way.

As we have seen, when we take a child's eye view we are concerned with understanding not just children's thoughts, but also their feelings. The feelings that they create in us can be an important guide to what children themselves are feeling. The role of teachers' feelings in making sense of classroom events is a further essential dimension of the process of reflective analysis which we have not as yet examined, and this aspect will be taken up in the following chapter.

CHAPTER 6
Noting the impact of feelings

How are feelings influencing what we see and understand about the situation? What do they tell us about what the child or children are feeling? We need to ask ourselves: 'How do I feel about this?', 'How are my feelings shaping my judgement?' and 'What do my feelings tell me about what is going on here?'

Teaching is an emotionally demanding and frequently stressful activity. The feelings aroused play an important part in the unfolding dynamics of classroom interaction and in the sense that we make of classroom events. The fourth questioning move, noting the impact of feelings, is concerned with trying to identify the emotions we are feeling associated with particular classroom events, and using this awareness as a source of insight and understanding.

Taking conscious steps to acknowledge feelings can aid the process of thinking through teaching in two ways. It can help us to recognise how our feelings may be shaping our interpretations, perhaps predisposing us to make certain kinds of interpretations and block out others, and feelings are also a source of insight and understanding in their own right. This chapter examines both, drawing extensively on the work of Daniel Goleman (1996) whose influential book, *Emotional Intelligence,* is strongly recommended to readers who wish to pursue in more detail some of the ideas and themes relating to the interplay between the emotional and rational mind explored here.

Goleman distinguishes the different ways of identifying the 'emotional' mind and the 'rational' mind as follows:

The empathic understanding that someone's watering eyes means that she is sad, despite her words to the contrary, is an act of comprehending just as surely as is distilling meaning from words. One is an act of the emotional mind, the other of the rational mind.   (Goleman 1996: 8).

Both minds are important, complementary sources of understanding. They work together, informing, questioning and reshaping the insights provided by the other. 'The two minds, the emotional and the rational mind, operate in tight harmony for the most part, intertwining their very different ways of knowing to guide us through the world' (Goleman 1996: 9). Our ability to act sensitively and intelligently with respect to the various challenges presented by our daily lives is at its peak, Goleman suggests, when both minds are operating in harmony. It is impaired when the balance tips in one direction or the other.

Emotional influences on judgement

Given the emotional demands of classroom teaching, it is not always easy to maintain a balance. As Ros Frost's story (Chapter 4) shows, strong emotions can swamp our ability to think clearly, or predispose us to interpreting situations in negative ways. They can lock us into a single, inflexible view of the world or lead us to jump to unwarranted conclusions. At the same time, 'actions that spring from the emotional mind carry a particularly strong sense of certainty' (Goleman 1996: 291). We tend to defend our judgements and the actions stemming from them more fiercely when there are very strong emotions invested in them.

Of course, the feelings we experience in the course of teaching are positive as well as negative. It is worth spending time thinking about the emotions each of us regularly experiences in association with teaching and the kinds of situations that trigger them. Asking ourselves what, in the course of teaching, makes us feel pain, pleasure, approval, disapproval, anxiety, disappointment, anger, resentment, delight, hope, despair, under threat, at ease and so on can be another way of uncovering the norms and values omnipresent in our judgements. The behaviour and learning about which we feel, say, approval or disapproval conform to, or deviate from, certain underlying expectations and values. By exploring the basis for our feelings of approval or disapproval, we can become aware of, and re-examine, those underlying values. As well as social and cultural influences, our particular personalities, preferences and predilections shape those qualities and behaviours towards which we feel positive and negative feelings.

Paying conscious attention to feelings is necessary in order to fulfil our responsibilities towards pupils, because there is evidence that teachers' feelings towards students do impact on their judgements of the students' academic capabilities and needs. In one study, for example, findings suggested that teachers' judgements of pupils' academic potential, and consequently the learning opportunities which they made available, were influenced by their opinion that a child was 'a pleasure to teach' (Tizard *et al.* 1988: 172).

Personal feelings and ways of viewing the world affect both what we see and what we record as significant. In an interesting study of issues relating to the assessment of children with hearing impairment, Parlett (1991) noted that:

> a very orderly individual who tends to feel uneasy in the presence of disorder is more likely to notice – and perhaps to feel strongly about – individuals who appear to him or her to be untidy or disorderly. Other professionals, lacking this particular preoccupation, might not comment at all on the child's disorderly habits; they simply would not judge them to be sufficiently noteworthy – they might not even 'notice' them (in Schon 1991: 22).

Parlett argues that the personal constructs of the individual making the assessment can act as filters, so that certain definitions and attributions are introduced that are almost solely a product of the assessor's personal way of looking at the world. Taking note of our feelings, then, can help us to check out if and how we might be filtering the 'evidence', and in the process open up a broader and richer picture of children's learning upon which to base the exploration of new possibilities for development.

Responding to a reluctant learner

When strong emotions are aroused in our relationships with children, they can block our efforts to think clearly and find a constructive way forward. This was powerfully illustrated by the experience of Ülfet, one of the teachers in our Enfield research group, when she was supporting Sezer, a 12-year-old boy of Turkish Cypriot heritage, in English and humanities classes. Usually she worked with Sezer as part of a group which included other Turkish speakers. Sezer's behaviour was causing great concern to all his teachers; Ülfet found that, even in a situation where she was able to give him her full attention, he would often resist her help, and refuse to put any effort into the work at all. She tried everything she could think of: really making an effort to be patient with him, explaining the work for him, even offering to write for him, but nothing seemed to work.

One day, during a lesson on the rise of Protestantism in the sixteenth century, Sezer was being particularly resistant to her efforts, and Ülfet felt at a complete loss. She said: 'I did feel really angry . . . and I felt frustrated . . . you know (I thought) I'm making a special effort to help you and you're just refusing'. Ülfet's account of how she felt illustrates what Goleman describes as 'emotional hijacking': when our emotions are so strong that they paralyse our powers of clear thinking. She felt helpless, believing there was nothing she could do with her feelings as they were too strong and that whatever she tried she was just going to be confused.

It was hard for Ülfet to admit, even to herself, the feelings that she was experiencing because her rational mind censored them. She felt that it was not appropriate for a teacher to be subject to such reactions – she *ought* not to be experiencing them. Acknowledging them, however, was the first essential step to bringing them under control and using them positively as a resource for understanding the situation.

Rather than persisting with a strategy that clearly was not working for either of them, Ülfet decided to take some time out – she sat at the side of the room to think. As she focused on her feelings, she began to appreciate that at least some of the anger and frustration aroused by Sezer might be linked to pressures and stresses that she was currently experiencing more generally in her personal and professional life. She also wondered if there might be a parallel between what she was feeling and what *he* was feeling, if he too was feeling angry and frustrated and helpless. She started to see how her well-meaning support might be experienced as unwelcome pressure from his point of view, while his feelings and needs went unacknowledged: 'I was, like, pushing him and saying "Come on, get on with it! Do this . . ." I didn't ask him what do you want to do? What do you think? What is your difficulty?'

By acknowledging and reflecting on her feelings, Ülfet was able to step outside her own self-centred focus and consider the situation afresh. This, Goleman argues, 'opens the way to empathy, to real listening, to taking another person's perspective' (1996: 285). Ülfet decided that she needed to give Sezer time to talk, to explain to her how he was feeling and why he was behaving as he was in the lesson. As a result of their discussion, she discovered that Sezer was genuinely perturbed by the content of the lesson. As a Muslim, he did not feel comfortable learning about other religions. She was able to negotiate with him the legitimacy of the curriculum topic, in such a way that he became prepared, without coercion, to participate in the lesson.

This incident and its resolution shed light, for Ülfet, on the dynamics of her relationship with Sezer. It heightened her appreciation of the interplay between emotion and action for both herself and Sezer, realising how her own feelings, reflected in both words and behaviour, communicated themselves to Sezer – and vice versa – in a self-reproducing negative spiral (Figure 6.1).

Noting the impact of feelings was an essential prerequisite for recognising the dynamics at work, and taking the steps that would help to generate a more productive relationship (Figure 6.2).

As a result of these new insights, Ülfet felt that some genuine channels of communication had begun to open up between herself and Sezer, that the brick wall that seemed to exist between them had, at least in part, been taken down. Although there was still a lot to do, she also felt more confident about what to do to help him.

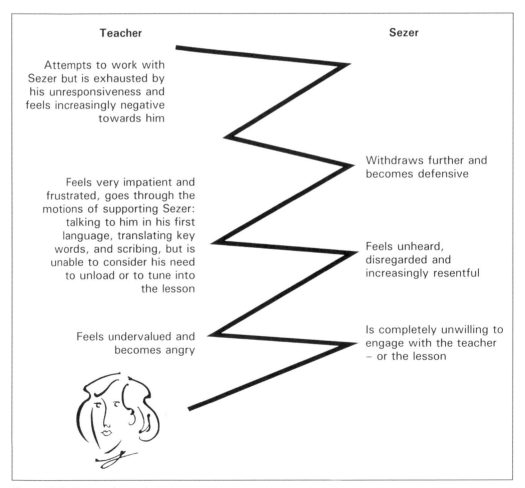

Figure 6.1 A negative spiral

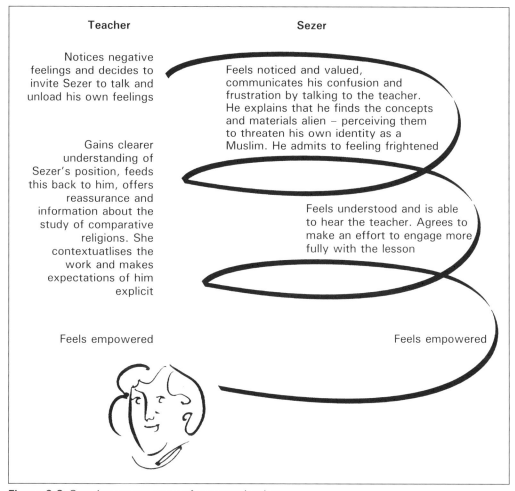

Figure 6.2 Opening up avenues of communication

I listened to him a lot. I spent about five or ten minutes nearly every session, before we started, I just listened to what he needed to say before I said anything to him or tried to explain the lesson to him. He needed to unload before he could take anything on board. I also began sharing some of my own experience because he was the kind of child that felt everyone else is OK, I'm the only one who can't do the work, or can't face the work.

Managing feelings

Ülfet's story shows that, when faced with a very challenging, emotionally charged situation, it may be necessary – indeed essential – to focus on feelings, and take steps to manage those feelings *before* any other approaches to reflective analysis are likely to yield productive results. Indeed, if feelings are ignored, the emotional mind may harness the rational mind to its own purposes, searching out evidence to confirm a particular view or interpretation that legitimates and fuels feelings, say, of hurt, anger or injustice that have been aroused.

The first essential step in managing feelings is to acknowledge what it is that we are feeling. This is not necessarily always straightforward. We may be aware of experiencing powerful emotions without necessarily being able to identify them. We may suppress or deny our feelings to ourselves (as Ülfet did at first) because they are too distressing to own up to, or because they conflict with our ideal image of ourselves. Some, less powerful, emotions can simmer below the surface without our even being aware of them. They may condition our response to events happening some considerable time later in the day, surprising us by the power of the feeling evoked by the second incident, because we are not aware of their link with the earlier event.

Once we have achieved conscious awareness of what we are feeling, it is important to take steps to manage those emotions. Goleman suggests two ways of achieving this. One, cognitive reframing, involves challenging the thoughts and beliefs that are triggering the surges of emotion. The idea is that if an alternative (preferably more positive) view of the situation can be thought of that strikes us as at least plausible, this will help to loosen the grip of the emotions that are tied to a particular interpretation of the situation. As Goleman argues, 'Seeing things differently douses the flames of anger' (1996: 60). This approach has already been examined in some detail in Chapter 4. The problem is that when we are in the grip of powerful emotions, we suffer 'cognitive incapacitation'. The stronger the emotions we are experiencing, the less able we are to draw on the resources of the rational mind to assist us in managing them. The second approach, allowing a cooling off period, can work if we can find a place in which there are no further triggers for the particular emotions aroused, and if we can find means of distracting ourselves sufficiently to alter our mood. It will not work if we use the time to fuel our emotions with further angry thoughts which serve to sustain, legitimate and at worst increase the hold of the emotions.

Ülfet used a combination of both these strategies. She gave herself the kind of cooling off period that her position as a support teacher allowed, and used it to think about her emotional response. She reframed the situation in two ways which were helpful in managing her emotions. First, she recognised that what she was feeling was due not just to Sezer's behaviour but also to external events and pressures that were nothing to do with him. Secondly, she tried to see the situation from his perspective, and began to realise that he might share many of the same feelings as herself. This empathic reframing was sufficient for her to bring her emotional and rational minds back into a more manageable balance, and to use both, in concert, to determine how best to move forward.

Teachers who are not in a position to take time out from their teaching in the midst of the action, can nevertheless make use of these strategies for managing feelings when reflecting on the lesson after the event. Many teachers, in my experience, do find themselves going over and over in their minds challenging situations that they have been facing. As Goleman says, 'Powerful emotions twist attention towards their preoccupations, interfering with the attempt to focus elsewhere' (1996: 79). However, not all of this mulling over necessarily leads to new insight and understanding. Indeed, as noted earlier, it can merely serve to reinforce an existing perception if the underlying feelings are not attended to and cared for.

Most important is to persist in the belief that, whatever the challenges the situation presents, some way forward can be found. Although Ülfet felt overwhelmed and helpless, she went on believing that progress was possible; that she would find some means of improving the situation with Sezer. The new insights she achieved did not lead to dramatic change, but they did open up new avenues of communication between herself and Sezer, helping to lay the basis for developing a more positive and productive relationship.

Drawing on the work of Seligman (1991) and others, Goleman insists that this basic attitude of optimism is essential if we are to be able to persist with a task in the face of constant setbacks and challenges. It is linked to a particular explanatory style – a way of explaining events – which places them within, not beyond, our control. It contrasts with an attitude of 'learned helplessness' where problems are explained in ways that imply they are not amenable to change (for example because they are due to our own inherent limitations, to the inherent limitations of others or to external events and circumstances beyond our control). Ülfet made an important distinction between blame and responsibility. She said, 'I did not blame myself, but I questioned myself. Looking into my feelings helped me to have a clear view of the child and the situation and I was able to understand him and start to think'.

Looking beyond the immediate situation

Part of what helped Ülfet to bring the situation under her reflective control was the recognition that unconnected external circumstances and pressures might be partly responsible for the feelings that she was experiencing with respect to Sezer. It is also important to consider the possibility that emotional reactions can sometimes be triggered by memories of emotionally charged events in the *past* that have some similarities with events of the present. There are many adults, for example, who find themselves feeling considerable emotional discomfort if called by their full, first name, because this is associated with being told off and incurring parental disapproval in childhood.

Adults who experience this are well aware of where their discomfort comes from. However, there are also likely to be many occasions in our daily lives when it is not at all obvious to us that emotional routines of the past are being re-enacted in the present. Since the trigger is always in the present, we associate our emotions with the events that immediately triggered them. In the grip of these emotions, we may attribute to the events in the present the same meaning that we associated with those emotions in the past. We misconstrue what is happening in the present, because we import into the present associations derived from our own personal and emotional autobiographies.

In psychoanalytic theory, this phenomenon is referred to as 'transference' (e.g. Greenhalgh 1994: 54). Transference is the process whereby we transfer feelings associated with situations and relationships with significant others (say with a parent or sibling) into other relationships and situations, and re-enact the feelings and relationships with others. So, for example, feelings of failure, frustration or powerlessness which I find myself feeling with respect to a child who does not seem to respond to my teaching may be a reflection of similar feelings felt as a child when my efforts to please my parents did not succeed in the way that I desired.

'Projection' and 'displacement' are further mechanisms that may be at work in our emotional responses. Projection is the process whereby we attribute to others thoughts, feelings and qualities that in fact relate to ourselves. For example, what I perceive as a child's hostile attitude towards me may be a projection of my own (unacknowledged) hostile feelings towards him or her. In displacement, we take out our feelings of anger, hurt, injustice or whatever other powerful emotion we are feeling upon someone or something other than the actual target of those feelings. Going home and shouting at one's partner, children or pets after a stressful day at work is one version of this. We may also find ourselves inadvertently taking out on our classes bruised feelings derived from a painful interaction with a colleague, or inflicting on our colleagues or family feelings of anxiety, threat and inadequacy aroused by particular pupils.

According to psychoanalytic theory, such mechanisms are universally present in human interactions, not just between teachers and children in classrooms and not just among those of us who are neurotic wrecks! To acknowledge this dimension of interpersonal relationships is important because it allows us, without denying the legitimacy and power of our feelings, to separate them out from the individuals with whom they seem to be associated in the immediate situation. In that way, we can create some new emotional space within which to take a fresh look at the situation, and avoid recourse to defensive strategies which would close off opportunities for further learning.

Feeling as a way of knowing

However, the issue is not simply to bring our emotions under control so that the rational mind can think clearly. Ülfet explained how, once she had achieved control over her emotions, she was able to use them as a source of insight and understanding in their own right. Having created the emotional space to reflect upon the situation more calmly, she was able to gain a fresh perspective on the origins of her own emotions and use these to try to attune herself to the emotional experience of the boy. 'Empathy builds on self-awareness; the more open we are to our own emotions, the more skilled we will be in reading feelings' (Goleman 1996: 96).

In Goleman's work, as in the literature on counselling, empathy is the term used to describe one of the key ways of knowing of the emotional mind. Greenhalgh (1994) describes what is involved as follows:

> Empathy is the function by which we attempt to perceive and understand what is happening in other people. Empathic understanding concerns being able to appreciate what life is like for the other person, understanding the other person's frame of reference, how the other person sees situations, relationships and the world in which s/he lives. It involves being figuratively able to stand in his/her shoes whilst remaining in one's own.
> (Greenhalgh 1994: 87)

As noted in Chapter 2, empathy is a form of awareness, not a process of rational analysis, and is another means of taking the child's eye view, as discussed in the previous chapter. It involves tuning in to the experience of the other through attention to feelings rather than through rational thought.

A capacity for empathy is important for teachers, since the rapport that they build with their classes determines the quality of learning that can take place. Empathy, or emotional attunement, is the means by which rapport is achieved. Throughout a teaching day, teachers will be using their empathic antennae to monitor the emotional climate of their classrooms, and the feelings of individuals within them. They will be reading and responding to the signs of their pupils' emotional states, most of which will be provided through non-verbal signs: 'People's emotions are rarely put into words; far more they are expressed through other cues. The key to intuiting another's feelings is in the ability to read non-verbal channels: tone of voice, gesture, facial expression' (Goleman 1996: 97).

Empathy also involves monitoring the impact of our own behaviour on others: being attuned to the impact of what we say and how we say it on the person who is on the receiving end. Such understanding allows teachers to make adjustments to their own words and behaviour, and to choose ways of being and relating which help to encourage the kinds of responses that they intend and desire to achieve in their relationships with their pupils.

When we are thinking through teaching, then, it is important to make use of our capacity for empathic understanding as one important source of insight into the situation that we are reflecting upon. We can replay in our minds students' non-verbal responses and review our own intuitive reading of their meanings; we can review our own behaviour and its affect upon the emotional climate or upon responses of individuals.

Feelings as a mirror of learners' feelings

Because empathy involves tuning into the feelings of others, it may lead us to experience ourselves the same feelings that others are experiencing. This can be frightening, even overwhelming, if the feelings are very strong. It can trap us into self-defence or retaliation, unless we are aware of the dynamics at work and can recognise our feelings as a possible clue to what our pupils are experiencing. It can happen in relationships between adults, as well as between adults and children (Salzberger-Wittenberg *et al.* 1983). Attending to our own feelings can be a particularly important source of insight when working with emotionally troubled children, as Greenhalgh explains. He acknowledges that one of the most challenging dimensions of such work for teachers is managing the feelings that children arouse in us.

> When working with disturbing children one might find oneself feeling hurt, abused, angry, frustrated, intolerant, anxious, deskilled and even frightened . . . Sometimes it might feel as if it is difficult to know where the feelings are coming from, and the intensity of them might lead one to question one's own competence and professional worth. The task is to look in detail at behaviour as a form of communication and expression of feelings.   (Greenhalgh 1994: 53)

He explains how awareness of the processes of projection and transference discussed earlier can help teachers to understand the origins of these feelings in the children's emotional experience, and their behaviour as a way of communicating their feelings and needs that they are unable to communicate in other ways.

> A child without the inner resources to tolerate a difficult feeling, a capacity for reflection, and language to communicate, is likely to express the difficult feeling through unconsciously 'acting it out' thus making others have the feeling associated with the difficulty.   (Greenhalgh 1994: 54).

As an illustration, Greenhalgh describes his early relationship with John, an eight-year-old who had been referred by his school to receive help in a tutorial class.

> During his first few months of twice-weekly attendance in a tutorial class group, John had a series of temper tantrums in which his anger and hatred were intense. During these tantrums he not only abused me, but screamed that he was not going back to 'that shit school', and on one occasion, that he wanted to put himself under a car. In the projection, I was made to feel as if I was in turmoil, not knowing what was happening to me, wondering if I could cope, and wishing I could give up and put an end to the suffering. I was made to feel something akin to what John was feeling. One of my readings of these events was that John had 'found' this way of communicating his feelings and that, at this point, he had at his disposal few other means of making such communication. (Greenhalgh 1994: 55)

It is vital for adults to be able to recognise these processes at work if they are to be able to manage their own emotions and provide essential emotional containment for the child's intolerable feelings such that change and development can begin to occur. One vital part of this is for the teacher to believe, to communicate to the child, and sustain on behalf of the child, a belief that the child will become less troubled. Teachers can only provide this kind of support for troubled students if they are able to bring their own emotions under control and use them as an opportunity to understand what is going on with the child.

However, we also need to take care that we do not mistakenly attribute to others feelings that are a product of our own psychic histories and needs. As noted earlier, we all bring our own emotional baggage into our relationships with others – including our professional relationships. Feelings of inadequacy and worthlessness aroused in a teacher by children's apparent rejections of her efforts to provide them with interesting, challenging work *may* be a clue to the children's own feelings, as learners, confronted with these well-intentioned activities. But they may also be triggered by association with the teacher's own childhood events. When we take time to note and reflect on feelings, it is important to give conscious attention to both sets of possibilities.

Summary

In this chapter, we have examined the distinctive contribution that noting the impact of feelings can make to the overall reflective process. The work of Goleman (1996) has provided an important resource for understanding the part that emotion plays in thinking and understanding. 'In the dance of feeling and thought, the emotional faculty guides our moment-by-moment decisions, working hard with the rational mind, enabling or disabling thought itself' (1996: 28).

We have seen how noting the impact of feelings can help us to understand:

- the part that our own feelings play in the dynamics of classroom interaction
- how our feelings shape what we see and pay attention to
- how our feelings affect the interpretations and judgements that we make
- the emotional state of pupils, including the emotional impact of our own behaviour
- the relationship between our own emotions and those of the children we teach.

In the process of thinking through teaching, then, it is important to pay attention to the feelings aroused by the particular set of events, individual or class that we have chosen to focus upon. We need to ask ourselves what the feelings are; what part they played in whatever took place; how they influenced our action at the time; and how we might use them now as a source of insight into what was going on. We do not do this in isolation but in conjunction with the workings of the rational mind, so that we are able to call on all our resources simultaneously to help arrive at an understanding upon which we feel confident to base further action.

In situations where strong emotions are aroused, it will be necessary, as we have seen, to attend to the emotions first before we can think constructively and analytically about a situation. At such times, the support and collaboration of a trusted colleague will be very important to help restore an emotional balance and sense of personal efficacy. To focus on feeling is not an indulgence; nor should we fear that in admitting to strong feelings we are exposing personal weakness. To acknowledge our feelings, and make constructive use of what we know about the part that feeling plays in understanding, is to increase significantly our powers of learning. To do so enables us to exploit more fully our power to make a difference to children's participation and learning.

CHAPTER 7
Postponing judgement

'Postponing judgement' entails deciding to hold back from the attempt to arrive at conclusions about what is happening, and about what needs to be done, while we take steps to acquire further information/resources. We ask ourselves: 'What more do I need to know?' and 'What shall I do to find out?'

Although there is always pressure on teachers to move rapidly from reflection to action, there are some circumstances when it is not a good idea to press ahead with the analysis. Sometimes questions come up that alert us to the need for further information. Sometimes in an unfamiliar or challenging situation, we may doubt the relevance of our existing experience and expertise; we may see a number of possible ways of interpreting a situation but are not sure which to pursue; and sometimes our efforts to think innovatively may simply run into an impasse and we cease to be able to generate new ideas. In all these circumstances, the wisest move is to postpone judgement: to take a conscious decision not to attempt to reach a conclusion at this stage, but rather to take steps to learn more and to obtain whatever additional information seems to be required.

This fifth questioning move complements and challenges the other four moves. It draws attention to the limits of our existing knowledge and prompts us to consider their implications. In this way, it safeguards the interests of children by helping to ensure that we do not jump too soon to conclusions that are not warranted by the information available. It also plays an important role in maintaining a sense of optimism, a belief that a way forward can always be found even in the most challenging of circumstances.

In this chapter, I explore the uses of this fifth move in more detail by examining some situations in which teachers have chosen to postpone judgement for various reasons. I look at what form the follow-up inquiry took in each case, and how the new information acquired helped to reshape their perception of the situation and what needed to be done. I consider why it is essential to include postponing judgement as an integral element of the framework for innovative thinking, and how this seemingly impractical strategy can be tailored to fit the busy, pressurised world of schools and classrooms.

Recognising a need for more information

Questions that alert us to the need for more information can arise at any point in the analysis, including right at the beginning. In the Enfield research, teachers chose to postpone judgement when questions arose concerning pupils' perceptions and feelings, about their experiences at school, about pupils' responses in different contexts, and about pupils' histories, backgrounds and lives outside school.

Finding out more about pupils' perceptions and feelings

As we saw in the previous chapter, part of Ülfet's strategy in trying to understand Sezer's resistance to her efforts to support his learning was to talk to Sezer and find out what the situation looked and felt like from his point of view. She realised that she had been trying to provide academic support without giving sufficient attention to the emotional dimensions of Sezer's learning. Following the humanities lesson described, she decided to find out more about Sezer's feelings about his school experience generally.

One activity she tried was to provide 'feelings cards' (see Figure 7.1) in Turkish, which Sezer sorted and discussed, saying if particular feelings did or did not apply to him, how often and in what circumstances. Sezer responded very well to this activity; he seemed to be excited to be asked to talk about his feelings and was well able to articulate how he felt about different aspects of school life, including his relationships with teachers and peers. The information enabled Ülfet to reorganise her support timetable so that she was able to observe and find out more about Sezer's learning specifically in those areas where he was experiencing particular difficulties.

Of course, not all teachers are in a position to work on a one-to-one basis, and not all learners would be comfortable to find themselves in the spotlight in such an intensive way. In their work with Asad (described in Chapter 8), Niv and Una suspected that they would not get very far trying to question Asad directly about his feelings and perceptions. Instead they created opportunities for discussion as part of normal learning activities. They used circle time activities as a way of exploring children's feelings about working in groups, about how groups were chosen, and patterns of inclusion and exclusion in friendship groups within the class.

WORRIED	DISAPPOINTED	INCLUDED
PLEASED	SAFE	SAD
INTERESTED	ENTHUSIASTIC	EXCITED
CLEVER	ANGRY	FRUSTRATED
ISOLATED	BORED	

Figure 7.1   Feeling cards (adapted from Ainscow *et al.* (1994))

Comparing children's responses in different contexts

Niv and Una also carried out some observations of Asad in various group situations in order to follow up various questions, arising from prior experience, about the kinds of situations in which he seemed to respond with most confidence. A similar strategy was used by two secondary teachers in the Enfield group, Karen and Gita, in the early stages of thinking about what to do to help a Year 7 Nigerian boy, Mohammed, in his English classes. Mohammed participated orally with great enthusiasm, humour and perceptiveness, but he was barely producing any written work at all. When he did put pen to paper, he would produce just a few words, apparently experiencing great difficulty with basic letter formation and simple spelling. What he wrote bore no resemblance to the wit and perceptiveness that he showed in his oral contributions.

Among the many questions that Karen and Gita found themselves asking about Mohammed's current abilities and prior experience, was how Mohammed responded to writing tasks in other areas of the curriculum. Was Mohammed's seeming reluctance to write in English something to do with *English*, as a subject, or the particular kinds of writing tasks that were set in English? Was it that he could write more, but was choosing not to? If they discovered that he wrote at greater length, and with greater facility, in other subjects, this would help to round out their perceptions of Mohammed as a learner and inform their assessment of his actual writing abilities. It would give them a firmer basis from which to interpret Mohammed's responses in English; and they could use information about activities and contexts that were more successful in encouraging him to write in other subject areas to help foster his writing in English classes.

As a support teacher, Gita was able to negotiate legitimately, as part of her role, the opportunity to shadow Mohammed for a day, so that she could see how he responded in other subject areas. Her observations confirmed that Mohammed produced little extended written work in other areas of the curriculum, so it was clearly not a problem that was unique to English. However, the experience did more than merely answer some of the questions that had been in the two teachers' minds. A day spent observing Mohammed and identifying with his perspective left her with a deep sense of frustration at the limited opportunities available for him to participate and express his ideas in lessons other than through literacy. She came away with a new agenda and a new set of questions about how to realise in practice the school's commitment to providing equal opportunities for learning for children, like Mohammed, who have difficulties expressing themselves through the medium of the written word.

As her experience illustrates, when we postpone judgement in order to gather further information, the new information obtained may change or broaden our perception of the issues as originally conceived. Some of our earlier questions may cease to be relevant, or we decide to move them to a back burner for the time being, while the new agenda is pursued. In deciding to pursue theirs, Karen and Gita were not abandoning their effort to support Mohammed with his writing. What they now saw more clearly was that Mohammed's writing development was not a technical problem which could be tackled separately from other aspects of school experience. If he was continually moving from lesson to lesson finding that he could not demonstrate, use and develop his abilities fully, then the frustration and sense of failure arising from this would undoubtedly affect his ability and willingness to undertake writing tasks and to respond to whatever help was provided for his writing. Moreover, there was a real danger that his abilities would be masked by his lack of literacy, and his frustration interpreted as laziness or disruptiveness rather than as an understandable response.

In planning work for Mohammed's class, as a priority they decided to extend their repertoire of activities to include more situations where participation and assessment were not dependent on well-developed literacy skills. They began to explore strategies that would encourage sophisticated thinking in response to a class text, while making only limited demands upon pupils' writing skills. As part of a unit of work on *Carrie's War*, for example, they used the 'fortune line' technique (White and Gunstone 1992) to encourage pupils to explore and debate key characters' emotional responses to events in the story (see Figure 7.2). Pupils had to read short phrases which acted as prompts relating to events in the story, and then discuss with a partner where the event came in the sequence (horizontal axis) and where to place it on a continuum of positive and negative emotional responses (vertical axis). The outcome was a fortune line that reflected the emotional ups and downs of the story, understood and interpreted by the pupils. Since pupils worked in pairs or threes, they needed to articulate their understandings to one another and arrive at a judgement about where to place each statement in relation to each axis. Pairs then compared completed fortune lines, looking for similarities and differences, and discussed the reasons for their differing responses.

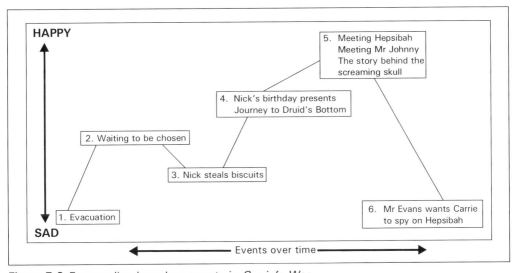

Figure 7.2 Fortune line based on events in *Carrie's War*

Carrying out the task in this way, rather than requiring individual written responses, gave Mohammed an equal opportunity to participate in the lesson and to demonstrate a sophisticated understanding of character and plot that he would have been unable to express through the medium of the written word.

The follow-up inquiry that led to this development work was made possible by the school's willingness to interpret Gita's support role flexibly and so enable her to gather information in contexts other than those where she was routinely present. Although it might seem impractical for teachers working with large classes to invest so much energy in thinking about one individual, it is evident that many other children in the same class also stood to benefit from the new strategies that Karen and Gita were prompted to introduce into their teaching. Indeed, it could be argued that there would be positive benefit for *all* the children to be derived from their teachers taking a fresh look at the quality and value of writing tasks set within a particular subject area, and extending the opportunities for learning and demonstrating learning other than through the written word.

Children's backgrounds and out-of-school experience

All the teachers in the Enfield research group decided, as a first step, that they needed to know more about the backgrounds of the pupils whose progress and learning needs they were studying. Conscious that bilingual children are by no means a homogenous group, they felt that they needed more background information about the children's linguistic histories, their prior educational experience, and the cultural values and practices of their homes. What they found out did provide important insights which assisted their efforts to understand and respond sensitively to their pupils' needs in the school context.

Ülfet, for example, discovered from reading past records that, part way through his primary schooling, Sezer had returned to Cyprus and been put back a year because he had forgotten a lot of his Turkish. Then, when his Turkish was gaining strength and his English fading, he had again returned to the UK and found himself in the same position again, this time in secondary school – having missed the transition from primary school. It was perhaps hardly surprising that he felt a deep sense of frustration and resentment at again being the outsider, coupled with shame at always being the one 'behind' everyone else, and that at times he gave vent to these feelings in school lessons.

Several of the teachers managed to organise home visits, and these also yielded valuable information. Karen and Gita, for instance, discovered that Mohammed was able to call on considerable support from his mother and sister at home. They developed strategies for supporting Mohammed's participation in lessons which made use of these valuable human resources, such as suggesting reading passages that Mohammed could prepare at home with his sister in advance of the lessons in which the passage would be read. Mohammed worked meticulously at these tasks, and was able to read aloud with great confidence and fluency in the following lessons, as well as offering assistance to peers who had not prepared the passages.

Accepting that it is not usually possible for busy teachers to undertake home visits, unless their responsibilities specifically allow time for this, it is nevertheless possible through a developing relationship with individual pupils, to gain access gradually to information about prior experience, cultural heritage and out-of-school activities. If teachers recognise the value of such information, then even the restricted opportunities presented by everyday interactions can yield useful insights which do make a difference. One secondary teacher, for example, picked up a great deal of information over the course of a year which helped her to ask new questions about a boy in her Year 7 English class, whose general attitude and behaviour she was concerned about. Through her conversations with Mohsin, Lesley gradually found out more about the religious beliefs, values and practices of Mohsin's home, the adult responsibilities which he capably fulfilled in his community, and the differences between the kinds of learning experiences that he encountered at school and at the religious school that he attended three evenings. This information suggested some possible interpretations of his behaviour that, without it, would not have occurred to her. Did he perhaps see school as a place for light relief from the more disciplined and solemn behaviour required of him by his religious practices? Did he have difficulty in taking seriously the kinds of work required of him by the school, because it was so different from the religious learning that he took part in outside school, and which was so highly valued by his community? Were her efforts to make learning 'fun' in fact creating problems for Mohsin because they departed too radically from Mohsin's perceptions of 'real work'?

Since Lesley was continuing to teach Mohsin the following year, she was in a position to pursue these questions and build on the understandings developed so far. In particular, she had become newly aware of problems that some of the curriculum topics planned might create for Mohsin because his Muslim background prohibited representation of human faces. She had noticed that he participated with great enthusiasm in projects about animals and objects, but when it came to people he seemed to disengage. Reviewing the topics planned, she realised that there were many which might unwittingly exclude Mohsin, and lead to ostensible behaviour problems if this went unrecognised. She needed to find out more about what was, and what was not, permitted and consider the implications of this for her curriculum topics. She realised, too, that this was not an isolated problem but one that needed serious consideration with respect to the appropriateness of the curriculum more generally for a culturally diverse student population.

As Lesley's experience confirms, whenever teachers are working with children whose religious, cultural, linguistic or social background differ significantly from their own, it is *always* relevant to ask 'what more do I need to know?' because there is always more to find out in order to reach a fuller understanding of children's responses to school experience. Access to research and literature is important here as a means of extending our knowledge beyond the limits of our cultural horizons. Insights provided, for example, by the work of Gregory (as discussed in Chapter 3), Heath (in Chapter 4), Tizard and Hughes (in Chapter 3) and Kiddle (in Chapter 5) provide the means to question features of the situation that we might not otherwise think to question, to appreciate barriers to learning that might not otherwise have come to our attention, to recognise possibilities for enhancing learning opportunities that might otherwise have escaped our notice.

At a loss to know what to do

Postponing judgement may also be the most productive strategy in situations where we feel at a complete loss. Even very experienced and competent teachers sometimes find themselves in situations where they simply do not know what to do. For example, Mary Jane Drummond (1995) tells the story of Janice Brown – a reception class teacher and deputy head of a first school – and Thomas, rising five, who seemed poised to create havoc in her previously well-ordered classroom. Janice recorded her first impressions of Thomas as follows:

> Thomas's fifth session was a Tuesday afternoon and he arrived in a very lively state; he ran shrieking extremely loudly across the room and then came back to where I was standing with his mother. I quietly tried to explain again about the way we enter a room, at which he ran and shrieked all the way across the room and back. He ran full force into me and thumped my stomach with his hands. Before I could say or do anything, Thomas's mother said 'He is so very excited about coming to school, he looks forward to it so much. He cannot understand why he doesn't come to school all day. I was wondering when he will be having an increase in sessions'. I felt like saying 'NEVER' but I refrained.

As Janice was currently undertaking a course on Early Years Care and Education as part of her study for an Advanced Diploma, she decided to focus on Thomas for her written assignment. Over the next few weeks, she continued to record observations of what she saw as Thomas's disruptive behaviour. Things did not improve. She wrote:

> In the early part of the term, if I asked him to sit down and join the others, he would refuse or go and sit somewhere else. If I asked him to do something quietly he would do it making a noise. If I asked him to walk, he would run, and if I asked him to run, he would walk. Thomas seemed to derive great pleasure in doing the opposite of whatever was suggested. He would laugh, smirk, smile; he would dance around singing loudly or even hold his hands in a 'claw position' and would hiss and snarl at myself or the other adults in the room. He would also be provocative in his spoken and body language.

Thomas's behaviour gave rise to a variety of feelings that Janice had to cope with in order to persist with her quest for understanding. Mary Jane Drummond (her supervisor) reports that: 'Though sometimes anxious, sometimes provoked, sometimes impatient, she continued to watch, to listen, to ask herself questions' (Drummond 1995: 116).

Then, towards the end of the first half term, an event occurred that provided the beginnings of a clearer understanding.

> We played a Look and Read card game. Thomas joined in well. Later when it was time to tidy up, Thomas began to throw the cards around. I said to him three times 'Don't throw the cards please Thomas, they will get damaged. If you damage the cards we won't be able to play the game again'. The other children in the group also protested and tried to stop him. Eventually, I said, 'If you throw the cards again, I will be very cross'.

Thomas just laughed and threw the cards in his teacher's face, asking 'How cross?' Janice was furious.

I shouted 'Very cross!' Everything went silent in the room. I had never shouted at any of the children before. Thomas looked shocked. The other children quickly picked up the cards with Thomas and put them in my lap.

Janice's initial reaction, as she wrote in her diary, was 'How dare this four-year-old question my authority?' But what happened subsequently caused her to question this interpretation and begin to see the situation differently. When Thomas returned after the half-term break, things seemed to have changed. Janice noted that 'he worked well, concentrated, played cooperatively with another child and tidied up when it was time to do so'. This incident, Drummond noted, and Thomas's subsequent behaviour, caused Janice to rethink what had been going on between herself and Thomas since the start of the autumn term.

Janice Brown explained how after she had shouted at Thomas, she had felt deflated, guilty, manipulated, dissatisfied with herself. And yet, in a sense, she felt she had answered Thomas with a new honesty. In the past, she had responded to Thomas's attempts to explore the boundaries of acceptable and unacceptable behaviour with professional self-restraint. While he was working, as it now seemed to her, with all his might, to find out how to enrage and infuriate her with transgressions of classroom routines, she had responded with the (almost) endless patience of the experienced reception class teacher. Her ability to keep calm, her refusal to get 'Very cross' had continually frustrated Thomas's attempts to understand how she worked and how she compared with the other adults he knew best. She realised, as she reflected on the incident, that for the first time since they met, she had been able to see an acceptable purpose in Thomas's deviant behaviour. Seeing Thomas not just more accurately, but more justly and lovingly . . ., entailed re-defining his non-compliance as systematic enquiry. Thomas did not share his teacher's interest in classroom rules and routines; his interest was in more volatile and immediate areas of experience – his personal relationships with adults and children. As a result of this internal act of re-definition, Janice Brown's own relationship with Thomas was radically changed.　　　(Drummond 1995: 117–18)

By keeping an open mind, while observing Thomas and her own response to him, Janice gradually reached a very different perception of what she had initially perceived as 'disruptive behaviour'. This reframing would not have been available to her earlier on, because it was only with hindsight that she was in a position to appreciate what might have been going on from Thomas's point of view. It was only when Thomas behaved differently, on his return from half term ten days later, that she was able to review the significance of his behaviour in the incident with the playing cards. Moreover, it was only from the evidence of how her relationship with Thomas evolved subsequently that she was able to give further grounding to her new interpretation of what had occurred.

Baffled by a child

Postponing judgement may also be an appropriate step when we encounter children whose patterns of development are very different from those of children we are used to working with. We may doubt the adequacy of our existing resources for making sense of children's responses to our teaching, or doubt our capacity for generating new ideas that we can use as the basis for subsequent action.

This was initially the case for Karen and Gita when they started working with Mohammed. His writing development appeared to be at such an early stage that, as teachers trained for secondary age pupils, they were unsure about the relevance of their existing expertise. Moreover, the discrepancy between Mohammed's perceptiveness and oral abilities on the one hand, and his difficulties with writing on the other, raised in their minds the possibility that he might be dyslexic. If that was the case, then what did it imply in terms of their teaching? Did they need specific knowledge and expertise in order to support Mohammed's writing development? Karen and Gita decided that they needed to develop their knowledge both about children's early writing development and about the needs of dyslexic pupils, so that this new knowledge would be able to inform their efforts to understand and meet Mohammed's needs. As we have seen, while they were pursuing these inquiries, Gita's experience shadowing Mohammed provided a new focus for their development work where they were confident about the relevance of their existing expertise. Nevertheless, they still continued their pursuit for additional knowledge of the processes of writing development.

I had a somewhat similar experience when I was researching children's writing development. I came across a child whose exceptional writing abilities forced me to recognise the limits of my existing ways of understanding and describing children's development as writers. The more I found out about nine-year-old Adrian's writing, the more I realised that I did not have a vocabulary or set of concepts with which to put into words the qualities of his writing that so impressed me. In my attempts to understand and describe the pattern of his writing development, I was unable to do justice to his writing abilities because I did not have the words to express the sophisticated understanding of how to use language to create particular effects that he was bringing to his work.

Not finding, in the literature, any ready-made frameworks for interpreting children's writing that appeared to apply to Adrian, my only option was to try to *develop* the understandings and concepts that were needed by studying Adrian's writing and talking to him about what he was trying to do. The full story of our work together is contained in the book based on this research (Hart 1996), and it would not be appropriate to go into it again in detail here. It is not put forward as a model for other teachers to emulate, because clearly classroom teachers are not in a position to work with one child intensively over a period of time in the way that I did. My purpose here is simply to help explain why postponing judgement has an essential part to play in our reflective repertoire. We need to take account of the possibility that, sometimes, in thinking through teaching, we may be confronted by situations where we do not have (or suspect we might not have) the experience or relevant expertise to be able to be confident in the conclusions of any analysis that we might carry out at a particular point. In that case, the most helpful course of action, in the interests of the children involved, may be simply to listen, watch closely, ask questions, find out more, learn from studying the situation what we need to know in order to understand and respond constructively to it.

In fact such an approach is generally regarded as good practice in early years education, where educators are keen to build up gradually a rich picture of each child's individual strengths, interests and needs, avoiding premature judgements of children's qualities and abilities made on the basis of scant evidence. It is also reflected in a moving account written by the personal assistant of a child 'with severe impairments' working with the child in a mainstream setting. Carol Sampson describes how an approach based on listening and learning helped her to see how the child might be more successfully included in the educational and social experiences of the whole group (see Figure 7.3).

For the past three years I have been supporting Claire, who has severe impairments, at St Simon's, her local community school. My experiences during this time have been both exciting and painful. Exciting because it has been a journey of discovery for us both.

Claire has discovered a life which many people who are disabled can only dream about. A place where she is accepted and valued for herself. She has real friends in her life for the first time. In the same way Claire has brought with her a gift for everyone at St Simon's; she has allowed them into her life which has made them so much richer for their experiences.

In the early days, I worked very hard on individual programmes with Claire, in the hope that one day she might be able to hold a cup, learn to feed herself or indicate physically what her needs were. I soon realised that this approach to her education did not bring encouraging results. I knew that I had to find another way, so I stopped trying to teach with a capital 'T' and started to listen.

Our roles were reversed. Claire became the teacher and I became the one who was to learn. She certainly does have her own way of communicating; all she needed was someone to listen to her. I stood back and watched the relationships develop with her friends in the classroom. They saw beyond her disability. Communication seemed quite natural for them. They have become confident in providing for Claire's additional needs and include her in all their activities as a matter of course.

Now, the class teacher and I work together to include Claire in most areas of the school's curriculum, adapting the work to suit her educational needs. Of course, inclusion is not an easy option and there are problems to contend with, but this simply means that we have to work that much harder and be that much more creative in order to discover the solutions.

Claire may never be able to hold a cup by herself, but that doesn't matter any more, because her friends will make sure she never goes thirsty. These friends are the key to Claire's future and through them both her parents and I will achieve our dream and Claire will have the opportunity to live a full life.

Figure 7.3 From 'Our journey of discovery' by Carol Sampson, Claire's PA

An essential role

This fifth questioning move helps to safeguard the interests of children by encouraging us to stop and think about the adequacy of the information that we have available to draw upon in making our judgements. By continually posing the question 'Do I know enough?', it provides a constant reminder of the inevitable limits of our personal resources. It forces us to confront the question of whether we know *enough* to have confidence in any conclusions reached in our analysis, accepting that we will always, inevitably, be working from information that is incomplete, and with experience and expertise that is always developing.

Postponing judgement plays an important role, then, by drawing attention to the inherent uncertainties associated with the reflective process. No matter how carefully we have thought things through, there will always be features of the situation that we have overlooked because it is impossible for any analysis to be exhaustive, no matter how much time we have available. The problem is, of course, that often we do not know what questions we need to ask. We do not know how our existing ways of seeing are constraining our capacity to understand a particular situation until new information becomes available that enables us to construe it differently.

Earlier on in this chapter, we saw how access to new information enabled a secondary teacher, Lesley, to start asking new questions about the impact of her teaching and about barriers within the curriculum that would not previously have occurred to her. In Chapter 5, we saw how the development of schema theory made it possible for parents and educators to understand children's behaviour in early years settings in a new way. Behaviour which previously was viewed with some concern because children seemed to flit from one activity to another, without any obvious connection between activities, suddenly could be understood as a reflection of genuine intellectual enterprise. Schema theory provided a means of recognising continuities underlying children's choices of activity where previously none had been discernible; it provided a means, for instance, of reinterpreting children's propensity for throwing objects and pouring liquids in undesirable places as a scientific quest for understanding rather than naughtiness on the part of the child (Easen *et al.* 1992).

So, even when we are confident that we do know enough to carry an analysis through to soundly based conclusions, we still need to be alert to the possibility that children's responses may be highlighting some features of the situation as yet unknown or inaccessible to us. However carefully the analysis has been carried through, conclusions must always be regarded as provisional. We need to keep an open mind, and be prepared to review and revise judgements already made in the light of fresh evidence and information becoming available. Possibilities that were previously excluded may suddenly seem relevant. Information that was available but not actually used on previous occasions may later be seen to have helpful insights to provide. Discussion with others may enable us to see possibilities that previously passed unnoticed.

To accept that uncertainty is an inherent and inescapable feature of the process of thinking through teaching is a cause not for dismay but for optimism. If there is no certainty, then there is always scope for learning. We can reasonably and legitimately hope that, through our continual efforts to understand, new insights will emerge which will enable us to reach out more successfully to include and involve all pupils. Meanwhile, our current state of knowledge is a position of strength, not deficiency. As Mary Jane Drummond explains, with reference to the work of Vivien Paley (discussed in more detail in Chapter 12):

> Paley is not dismayed or destroyed by the necessity of reshaping her interpretations of children's thinking. For Paley, as for all of us, knowledge is always 'from a position'. The new 'position' from which she applies her knowledge of children's minds may in turn be reformed and renewed; in the meantime, there is no weakness in her understanding, but a strength, in that as she strives, in her daily work, to understand what she has seen, she also constantly and critically reviews this very process of coming to understand.   (Drummond 1993: 74)

Conclusion

Part Two of the book has looked in detail at what is involved in using each of the five moves that make up the framework for innovative thinking. In each chapter, I have tried to clarify what is distinctive about the perspective offered by each move, and how each in its specific way helps to safeguard children's interests. I hope that these five chapters will have proved useful to readers in reviewing their own stores of knowledge about teaching and learning in schools and classrooms, and in making links between this knowledge and the use of the five questioning moves. I also hope that this section of the book will have provided an empowering sense of how much scope there is for asking questions about classroom events, for probing more deeply into what occurs, and for drawing more extensively upon our existing knowledge and expertise in reviewing and reflecting upon our teaching.

Of course, time is always teachers' enemy – there is only very limited time that can be invested in reflection of this kind, given current conditions in schools. I hope, too, that, by drawing attention to the scope that exists for enhancing children's participation and learning when teachers regularly and routinely reflect upon their practice in the ways suggested in this book, a convincing case can be put forward for more time, opportunity and encouragement to be made available to teachers to engage in innovative thinking.

With this aim in mind, Part Three of the book provides detailed accounts of the kinds of developments in thinking and practice that came about for some of the teachers in our Enfield research group as a result of using the framework to support their own thinking about individual children who were giving cause for concern. One is set in a primary school, the other in a secondary school. Both illustrate the application of the various moves in specific contexts, and show how the insights that emerged were used to guide the development of practice. Both illustrate how this focus on individuals can be used to the benefit of all pupils, and contribute the development of education generally.

PART THREE

CHAPTER 8

Including Asad
Niv Culora and Una Pattrick

It is not often that teachers have the luxury of standing back and keeping a journal! For us, a mainstream teacher and section XI support teacher working in partnership in a Year 4 class, the opportunity arose when we used the framework for innovative thinking as part of a research-based in-service course, designed to explore ways of enhancing the participation and learning of a bilingual pupil in our class whose learning was causing us concern.

We chose to focus on Asad, whose response to a lesson on the Spanish Armada has been discussed in earlier chapters. Over the period of a year, we thought carefully about Asad's engagement in the classroom as a learner. Using the framework for innovative thinking as a basis, we reflected on existing provision, and tried out and reviewed new ideas and strategies. As part of this we kept a journal. In it, we recorded our thoughts and feelings about Asad's learning, the action we proposed to take, the impact we felt this action was having on the pupil and any other significant observations. We also recorded any comments made by the pupil that we felt needed to be probed further.

In this chapter, we explain what we did and learned as a result of our focus on this particular pupil, using extracts from our journals to illustrate how our thinking and practice evolved. We put most emphasis on practical developments, which we believe benefited not just Asad but the whole class, because we anticipate that teachers will be most interested to know how our reflections actually informed the ongoing development of our work.

Background

We work in a large, multicultural and multilingual primary school in North London, with over 700 pupils on roll. Over 40% of these pupils are of diverse ethnic backgrounds, with the largest groups being Black Caribbean and Turkish. There are few pupils of Asian background, only 11%, and within this group only ten pupils are of Bangladeshi origin.

Why we chose Asad as our focus

Asad was born in Bangladesh and had been in UK education since nursery. When we first met Asad in Year 2, he was very chatty, keen to have a go at everything and used both English and Bengali in the classroom. He enjoyed books and, with the help of picture cues, was beginning to tackle text. Although not an independent writer (he was only copy writing) he had some good ideas that he shared. Socially he was happy and had a firm friendship with another Bengali boy, Roni, with whom (during Year 3) he spent all his time at school and some time outside school. This relationship seemed to boost his confidence in the classroom and Roni gave Asad the support he needed with his learning.

In Year 4, the classes were mixed up and Asad was separated from Roni. This separation drew our attention to the difficulties that Asad seemed to experience without Roni to help him and we began to be concerned about his progress. Socially Asad's spoken English was good but he interacted very little with his peers and had not made close relationships with any other child in the class. As a result he was often on his own during the school day. Asad had made some progress in literacy. He was developing strategies to tackle a number of fiction texts and his spelling was improving enabling him to become more independent as a writer. However his writing tended to be unstructured and at times it was difficult to follow his thinking. In teacher-led group work Asad was chatty and willing to take part but we were concerned because it often appeared from his contributions that he had not grasped the content of the lesson.

Learning more about Asad

We decided that we would use the innovative thinking framework to inform ourselves about Asad's needs and help us to decide on effective ways forward. We chose to start by postponing judgement, in order not to jump to conclusions until we knew more about Asad's learning and personal circumstances. Our initial meeting was spent brainstorming what we already knew about Asad and what other information might be useful. We made a map of possible routes to explore (see Figure 8.1). We decided that one important step, that we could readily put into operation as part of our normal teaching, was to carry out some classroom observations in order to gain a more detailed understanding of Asad's classroom experiences.

During the lesson on the Armada referred to previously, we were observing Asad in order to find out what he really did during a lesson and if he would make use of any strategies we put in place to support his learning. One of us observed Asad and kept detailed notes of his participation during this lesson, while the other presented the lesson.

The pupils were given a number of sources to work from including paintings, a video extract and contemporary written extracts. We wanted pupils to come up with a list of reasons why the Armada failed, using the sources and drawing on skills we had worked on in previous lessons. We also put in place other supportive strategies for Asad and

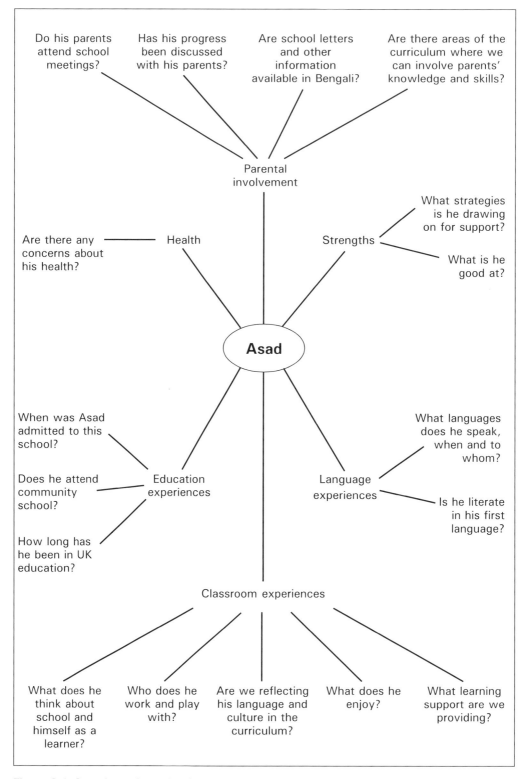

Figure 8.1 Questions about Asad

other pupils. We structured tasks and provided recording grids; we used visual materials; we encouraged collaborative discussion and working in a small group or with another pupil.

Our journal entry reveals our disappointment at Asad's response to the task and with his account of what he had learnt (see Figure 2.2 on page 11).

> 26. 11. 96
>
> Asad didn't appear to be interested in the introduction. He stood up sat down and generally looked around the room. He hardly contributed and when he did his answers were unrelated to the topic. When the task was set he took a long time to settle and he made no attempt to discuss with his group. His verbal responses were also disappointing as he didn't include any of the points we were expecting as answers to the question 'Why did the Armada fail?'

The journal also records some of the questions that we began to ask ourselves about this lesson that led to a shift in perspective:

> Perhaps our expectations aren't realistic? Does Asad have the language or knowledge to produce this piece of work? Has he understood the question or is his understanding of it different? Did we make our intended outcomes clear? Was he reluctant to take part or just not ready to commit himself? We have been anxious about his learning. What messages are we communicating to Asad about our disappointment? Might he see himself as a failure?

Contradicting

When we looked again at the lesson and the resources we had used, we concluded that Asad's response was not so disappointing after all; rather it was inevitable in the circumstances. Although we felt that we had put lots of support in place, in fact we had not put Asad in a position where he could draw effectively on his existing knowledge and skills to support his learning. The language of the written sources was too difficult; they demanded reading and language skills that Asad didn't have, and were written in a style unfamiliar to Asad and to most of the class. The lesson was also too long, with too many aspects, and we were asking the pupils to do too much in one go. The task assumed that the pupils would have an understanding of battles and ships and weather and the importance of leadership, concepts that needed to be developed to tackle the task successfully. There was very little that Asad, along with many other pupils, could relate to his prior learning and experience.

On the positive side, though, there were lots of ideas here which we could use to help us think how to foster Asad's learning more successfully through subsequent work. We decided to focus our efforts on using these ideas to develop the learning environment in ways that would more effectively harness Asad's strengths as a thinker and learner.

Making connections

Our current understanding of the conditions that help to create a supportive learning environment for all the pupils in multilingual classrooms was guided by the six aspects of the learning environment defined by our Language and Curriculum Access Service (1995) in the publication *Making Progress* (see Figure 8.2). LcaS believes that 'the Learning Environment is the key to the progress of bilingual pupils, and all pupils, and that it is always under teacher control'. It is the way we define and organise the learning environment that has an impact on the participants: how they view themselves as learners; how they build on what they know; how they interact and consider information together; and how they demonstrate understanding.

We used the conclusions arising from the Armada lesson to review key areas of the learning environment, formulating specific questions relevant to Asad that might help us to enhance his participation and learning. These were some of the questions that we decided to use to help us in future planning:

Curriculum content and planning
- Is there the opportunity for Asad to draw on and share his learning and cultural experiences?
- Have his language and curricular needs been taken into account?

Teaching approaches
- Do the approaches enable Asad to participate fully and demonstrate what he knows?
- Is the task presented in the most effective way?
- Are instructions and explanations meaningful to him?

Resources and materials
- How accessible are the resources in terms of language?
- Do the resources reflect his language and cultural experiences?

Identity
- Does classroom work give Asad a sense of satisfaction and achievement?
- Does classroom work communicate to Asad that his contribution is important and valued?

We summarised our current priorities for development work as follows:

January 1997
The Tudors unit of work did not offer the scope for Asad to show the extent of knowledge he is bringing to his work. We're concerned about Asad's self image and confidence in the class and realise there is also a need to help raise his status and his identity in the classroom. We want to find a way for him to be in the position of expert within the group. We want the whole class to recognise and value this expertise. We also want to match new learning experiences to prior experiences so that Asad will hopefully engage more readily with the curriculum by sharing his knowledge with others.

ADMISSIONS	Are the school's admission procedures effective?	• Was the parents' first contact with the school welcoming and friendly? • Have we established what interpretation and translation services we need? • Do we have full and correction information, or should we seek further information? • Has the pupil been placed in the most supportive context? Are there speakers of the same language in the class? Are there established welcome routines such as class friends?
IDENTITY	Does the pupil feel valued valued as an individual with a home language, culture, life experience and intellect?	• Am I sure I know the correct pronunciation for the pupils' names? • Do I know what languages my pupils can speak, write and understand? • Is the pupil encouraged to share out of school experiences and aspects of home life? • Have I established my role as a listener? • Do we have effective procedures for dealing with and challenging intimidation – particularly all forms of racism?
CLASSROOM MANAGEMENT	Does my classroom management ensure the confident involvement of bilingual pupils?	• Does the child feel safe? • Are my classroom routines consistent and explicit? Will a newcomer be able to identify and use them easily? • Do I enable pupils to work in different groups to encourage social cohesion? • Do I provide opportunities for pupils to use their first languages with each other? • Do parents/carers feel welcome in my classroom? Do I provide opportunities for parents to discuss any issue concerning their child?
CURRICULUM PLANNING	Does my planning take into account the pupils' needs and curricular needs as they are bound together?	• Do I plan clearly defined and staged tasks which are purposeful, practical and geared towards the pupil's experience? • Do I plan for collaborative work with visual and contextual support? • Are the tasks defined to encourage involvement and contribute to the work of the class as a whole? • Do I recognise that pupils will need opportunities to listen, tune into and absorb English before they are ready to speak? • Do I recognise the importance of talk in my planning? • Do I provide opportunites for talk with a range of pupils who will act as fluent models of English? • Do I provide opportunities for pupils to discuss in their own first language? • Do I structure a supportive print environment with writing related to the current topic/theme/area of study available? Is it clearly visible? • What importance do I place on pupils' writing in their first language?
RESOURCING	Are pupils' languages, cultures and experiences reflected in resources?	• Have we provided resources that support independent learning including material in dual or first language? • Do pupils have easy access to bilingual dictionaries? • Do the pupils know where resources are kept and have easy access to them? • Have we recognised the importance of visual aids – video/audio tape/pictures/photos/posters/illustrated wordbanks/charts and diagrams – to support understanding?
TEACHER/ PUPIL INTERACTION	Are my interactions with pupils effective in promoting learning?	• Do I value, promote and defend the pupils' rights of identity in the classroom? • Do I monitor the tasks I provide, the way I present them and the effectiveness of my interventions in relation to the pupils' performance? • Do my actions clearly show empathy? A smile often says a lot.

Figure 8.2 The Learning Environment (Language and Curriculum Access Service (1995))

Planning to include Asad

We started by considering the strengths and the experiences Asad would be able to share in the classroom. We then looked carefully at the term's curriculum focus and we planned for activities and strategies that would enable Asad to share and build on his linguistic and cultural experiences, and in turn have a positive effect on his learning.

Curriculum content

Fortunately, the following term's unit of work was on India, and we were able to adapt it with relative ease. In order to encourage more meaningful and successful learning we extended the topic to include Bangladesh and Pakistan, while still meeting the national curriculum requirements by developing geography skills.

Resources

We developed the reading corner to include stories and poems in English and dual texts from Bangladesh, Pakistan and India, as well as information books about these places. We listened to Bengali story tapes. Positive images were displayed around the classroom, and we used these as the basis for discussion work, and for comparisons between aspects of life in Britain and the other focus countries. Through homework based on research, we planned for the involvement and contribution of parents, by drawing on their expertise for information gathering and displays. We encouraged children to share their linguistic expertise by telling stories in their home languages and by developing captions for displays in the home language (e.g. labels, positive images, pictures). We were very heartened to see how Asad responded:

> February 1997
> Asad took the Bengali book and tape home to read and, for the first time ever, he came to school and read some Bengali poems to the class. The whole class responded by clapping and it seemed to give his confidence a real boost.

Teaching approaches

We developed various different kinds of grids, and charts with prompts, to help Asad record his thoughts and to make clear the purpose and outcome of the work. We also tried using writing frames (Wray and Lewis 1997) to provide him with a structure in which to organise his ideas. These various approaches (see Figure 8.3) really seemed to make a difference to the quality of Asad's participation in classroom activities. Asad became very interested in the topic from the onset. He took part in whole-class discussions and had lots of relevant things to contribute.

For example, in one particular lesson, pupils were comparing photos of street scenes. They had to use clues to work out where the photos were taken, and to be able to justify their decision. Asad took the lead in pointing out shop signs written in Bengali. He also supplied the information that it is hot in Bangladesh when it rains. He told the class

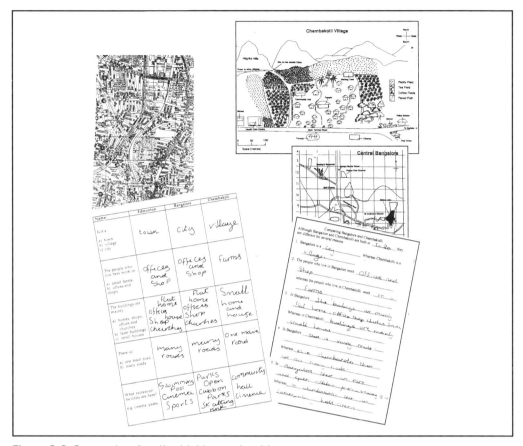

Figure 8.3 Supporting Asad's thinking and writing

'When it rains in Bangladesh it floods, but it's really hot and we go outside to play. It's called monsoons'. His body language suggested how important to him it was to be the information-giver.

Noting the impact of feelings

We thought afterwards about how, in this lesson, we were so delighted and encouraged to see Asad's contribution, that our feelings surely communicated themselves to him. We were reminded of our concerns, after the Armada lesson, that our feelings of disappointment might have communicated themselves to Asad and influenced his own feelings about his learning. The contrast between our responses in the two situations made us think more generally about the messages that we communicate to children – and to Asad in particular – through our responses to their learning. It made us more aware of our own body language and the effect that this can have on children's responses. Perhaps it was, in part, our increasingly positive feelings about Asad's responses to the various developments, communicated through our facial expressions and body language, that had helped to give Asad the confidence to make more contributions and to tell stories and poems to the whole class in Bengali.

Learning from Asad

While these encouraging developments were taking place, we were still aware, however, of tensions in Asad's relationships with other children, which had been an issue of concern since the start of the year. We were eventually prompted into action in this area by a comment Asad made during a parents' consultation evening. Asked if he wanted to say anything, Asad stated that he didn't like working in groups. As this was the first time that he had actively expressed dislike of anything, we felt that it must therefore be something that he felt strongly about. But when we were thinking about it later, we realised that we were not sure exactly what he was saying. Was he referring to the particular group that he usually sat with? Or did he mean *group work* generally?

The issue of Asad's relationships with other children in the group and the impact that these might be having on his learning had come up in the Armada lesson, when we were thinking about why he had chosen to work alone, but it had not been our major priority for development work until this particular situation allowed Asad to bring his feelings to our attention in this way. We discussed together how to respond, and recorded our thoughts in our journal as follows:

> March 1997
> He appears reluctant to join in discussions and often asks to work by himself. Earlier in the week, when groups were forming, he burst into tears. He often complains of a tummy ache just before group work, could this be anxiety? We need to find out what he feels about different parts of the day at school and to establish what it is about 'the group' that makes him unhappy.

We decided that we needed to look more closely into issues of grouping, and think more carefully about the groups that we encouraged Asad to work with. We were also interested that Asad had chosen to say this when his father was present. Had he chosen this occasion because he felt more secure? Because he had been given space to speak? This started us thinking about the conditions that encourage children to voice their thoughts and feelings. How safe do the children – and Asad in particular – feel to express their feelings about their school experience? Do they expect their thoughts and feelings to be heard, to be taken seriously?

Postponing judgement

Again, we decided to start by making some observations. The first observation was of Asad choosing a partner for a brainstorming activity. Asad took a long time to choose and some of the class made it clear they didn't want to be chosen by him. The second observation was during a PE lesson. The class was asked to get themselves into groups of four. Asad would not go to a group even if they were one short. He waited until a child took his hand and led him to a group. Subsequent observations showed that Asad was not chosen and left until last. This upset him, and on one occasion when the group's body language made it quite clear that he wasn't wanted by them, and that they were the unfortunate ones to have him, he burst into tears. Once in the group, Asad was excluded; he made no attempt to take part or to challenge the rest of the group.

Making connections

We also noticed at this time that, in teacher-led or in similar attainment groups, Asad appeared to be more confident. He took part in discussions offering ideas and personal opinions and relating discussion topics to his own personal experiences. His work following these sessions was of better quality than in other group combinations. In addition, we noticed that he spent time in the playground with these same pupils. We wondered if these other pupils were experiencing similar feelings about group work.

Taking a child's eye view

Although we actively encourage pupils to work collaboratively, Asad's comments and our subsequent observations made us realise that Asad was not experiencing the group as supportive in many cases. Looking at the experience of collaborative work through his eyes made us realise that if he was to make use of the learning opportunities presented by collaborative working, he needed to feel comfortable and valued within the group. In order for that to happen, we needed to work with the whole class to develop children's abilities to work productively together, listen to, value and build upon on one another's contributions.

Whole-class development work

As part of the curriculum for personal, social and health education (PSHE) curriculum, we decided to develop circle time (Mosley 1996) to explore relationships, set class rules and find solutions to individual and class issues. We felt that everyone in the class needed to have the opportunity to express feelings and opinions and the right to be listened to. In circle time, all pupils sit and listen attentively and non-judgementally to one another. This structure provides the chance for each child to share concerns and opinions in a supportive environment, and an opportunity to reflect on their actions, to take responsibility for their choices and make decisions.

The pupils responded well, and it became an important part of their week. The careful planning of circle time was important, and whole-class activities were always followed up by individual or small-group tasks. Even so, at first Asad seemed reluctant to take part in the whole-class forum. It occurred to us that his reluctance might mean that he was not ready to answer, when it came to his turn, first time round; and that he might feel more ready to contribute once he had heard everyone else. We tried giving people a second chance, and it proved to be helpful not just for Asad but for other quieter members of the class.

28 April 1997
Asad lacked confidence and put his hands over his face with embarrassment when he did not speak during circle time. At the end of circle time, I asked the children, if they hadn't contributed, would they like to join in now? Asad responded to this and was able to contribute to the circle time.

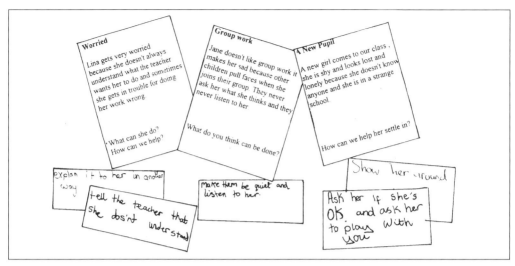

Figure 8.4 Activities contributing to the 'What Should We Do?' book

Each week, we worked on a different class issue, and at the end we produced a 'What Should We Do?' book for the class to refer to. We gave the pupils situations written on card to discuss together, such as how to help someone new to the school, or what to do if someone is always being left out of groups (Figure 8.4). In this way, we focused on issues of relationships and feelings, but without singling out individuals in a way which suggested that they had a problem. We also explored different ways of grouping children, and different strategies for creating groups (for example handing out coloured pieces of paper), and invited pupils to comment. As the groups changed frequently, and selection appeared random, the pupils were more accepting of one another.

In addition, we encouraged ourselves to listen more to the children by giving each child a personal journal, so that we could begin to communicate with them individually. Asad regularly took his journal home, and shared it with us. In it he wrote in Bengali, he wrote stories and he put a photograph of himself and his mother in it. He also wrote a lullaby and sang it to the class. This was a considerable personal achievement. We responded to the journal entries by sharing something about ourselves, and by always ending with an open question.

Developing our approach to history teaching

As we began planning for the summer term history topic, we realised that this could present the same sort of difficulties as we had encountered in teaching the earlier topic on the Tudors.

May 1997
The topic this term, as with the Armada, is beyond Asad's immediate experiences. We need to find a way of relating the topic to what he already knows and then building on that, thereby extending his experiences and knowledge.

Drawing on all that we felt that we had learnt about Asad, the class and ourselves, we worked out an alternative approach to the teaching of history that we hoped would be more successful. We knew that in order to support Asad's learning, we needed to:

- consider grouping and class organisation carefully so that he feels safe to contribute;
- relate the topic to his experience and prior learning;
- provide opportunities for all pupils to discuss key ideas through personal engagement with the task;
- model outcomes and language necessary to complete the task;
- offer different ways for pupils to show what they have learnt.

We identified key words, phrases and ideas that pupils would need to record their newly acquired knowledge and, drawing on circle time strategies, we modelled the appropriate language and the ideas that we wanted them to acquire. The class explored key facts, concepts and language through hot-seating and by acting out scenarios. Role play and hot-seating (where one individual, in role as an historical or fictional character, answers questions posed by the class), gave Asad the opportunity to clarify and articulate his ideas.

We gave particular attention to grouping, so that Asad had a defined role in a group, giving recognition to his contributions. Planned feedback discussions provided Asad with additional oral information reinforcing his understanding and supporting his writing. Again, writing frames gave him a structure to record his ideas and prompted the use of the required genre.

In one lesson, for example, our objective was for the children to consider whether Christopher Columbus should be funded for his expedition; and then to write a persuasive piece of dialogue, either as Columbus or Queen Isabella. By using the 'teacher in role' approach, we told the story and modelled the language they would need in order to complete the task, in this case persuasive language. The children then paired up and developed a short scenario, rehearsing the required language and information before attempting to write.

June 1997

We were pleased with Asad's response. He worked well with a partner and remembered the key events and points. He was able to complete the written task with confidence. We felt that this had been helped by the fact that the routine of circle time was familiar, the rule about careful listening, without distractions, was by now well established. The task was realistic and the amount of information manageable. The task was also within the children's experience and knowledge, i.e. arguing their point of view, making demands, being asked to give reasons.

We used drama to explore other concepts and develop empathic understanding, such as a sense of what it would have been like to be a cabin boy on one of Columbus's ships. This time, the whole class was involved in the drama, as the cabin boys on the ship. Again using the 'teacher in role' approach, this time as the captain and as a cabin boy, we shared relevant information with the children through hot-seating, by giving them the opportunity to ask us questions in role. As the new crew, the pupils mimed the jobs on board ship. We developed the drama by introducing conflicts at different intervals during the journey and asking pupils to share their feelings about the events.

These lessons helped to enhance the learning of the whole class, and particularly the quality of their writing. Asad also wrote an informed and empathic diary entry as a cabin boy on Columbus's ship (see Figure 8.5).

Conclusion

The innovating thinking framework encouraged us to question each situation and look at it in different ways, and to find out more before jumping to conclusions or deciding what support strategies to adopt. We realised that the support strategies that we had originally introduced were not sufficiently supportive for Asad, because we had not really known enough about Asad before putting them in place. Through continually reviewing and reflecting upon Asad's responses, we were gradually able to achieve a better match between what we knew about Asad as a learner and the kinds of support strategies that would assist and foster his learning. Our focus on Asad also led us to consider whole-class dynamics and the impact that these have on children's learning. It heightened our awareness of the need to create opportunities for the children to be heard, and to create a climate in which they felt safe to air their feelings. Focusing on Asad provided a stimulus to thinking about particular issues of teaching and learning, that gave us new insights into the learning of all the children. It enabled us to develop approaches, strategies and resources that we believe enhanced the learning of the whole class.

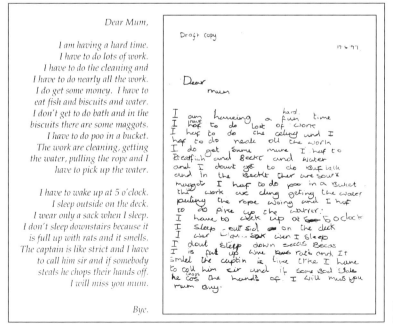

Figure 8.5 Asad's diary entry (draft)

CHAPTER 9

Involving Ayse
Lesley Higgs and Penny Travers

This chapter is an account of work carried out in a Year 7 English class by a subject teacher and language support teacher, working in partnership to explore ways of involving Ayse, a girl of Turkish heritage, more fully in lessons. The account has been prepared jointly, but has been written in two parts in order to try to maintain our individual perspectives. In the first part, Penny (the advisory teacher) focuses specifically upon how our thinking and practice evolved through our partnership work with Ayse and her class. In the second part, Lesley (head of English) focuses upon how she has used the framework for innovative thinking, and other ideas arising from our partnership work, in other situations.

Background

The school is a large multilingual comprehensive of approximately 1400 pupils, 41% of whom (at the time of carrying out this research) are bilingual. The term 'bilingual' refers to pupils who have access to, or need to use, two or more languages at home and at school. Between them, these pupils speak 47 different languages, Turkish being the language spoken by the largest number. Within this Turkish-speaking group there are both second and third generation children, many of Cypriot origin, and some newly arrived in the UK mainly from the Turkish mainland and from the Kurdish community, as in Ayse's case.

Why we chose Ayse as our focus

We chose to look closely at Ayse's learning because she seemed to be the sort of learner who is easily overlooked in the classroom. She was always very polite, helpful, friendly and well behaved; she was clearly seeking to please us as teachers by offering to help with classroom tasks and routines. But once lessons were under way, she seemed to glaze over; it was as if her mind was elsewhere. The challenge for us was to explore whether we could go beyond categorising Ayse (either explicitly, on record, or – perhaps more damagingly – simply in our own minds) as uninterested/unable, and find ways of supporting and fostering her learning more successfully.

Ayse had been identified at her primary school as having difficulties in learning literacy. Her primary records indicated that she had scored low results on reading and spelling tests and that she had 'difficulty listening to instructions and explanations'. They also noted that her first language was Turkish and that she was at the progressive range of learning English. Pupils in this range have moved beyond the initial phase of English language acquisition and 'are faced with making themselves understood within the expectations of academic work' (LcaS 1995).

Ayse, then, arrived in Year 7 to face the demands of the secondary curriculum which are complex and text based, and in a language which is not her mother tongue. In her Year 7 interim report, one teacher commented that she 'tries very hard, although she finds the work difficult'. Other subject teachers noted that she had 'difficulty in getting started and keeping going . . . in concentrating . . . doesn't try to understand'.

Learning through talk and reflection – Penny's story

Working with her as a support teacher at this time, I noted my own response to Ayse in my journal as follows:

> I see her as a child who, at a social level, is keen to engage – certainly with me and Lesley [her English teacher] – keen to please, not 'switched off' at all. However I'm worried about the fact that she doesn't appear to engage very much with the curriculum. I feel as though she goes through the motions because that's what the teachers tell her to do and that's what she sees other pupils doing but I don't have a sense of any of it meaning very much to her, of her making it her own.

Once my colleague, Lesley, and I had distilled, through discussion, our initial assumption that 'Ayse lacks involvement in learning', we decided to begin by taking steps to discover more about Ayse, to give ourselves time to think about her experiences as a learner before trying to reach any conclusions about what we might do to support her learning. We recognised that this was *our* perception of Ayse's response to school learning, and we wanted to find out more about what this response meant from her point of view.

Working in partnership gave us the chance to carry out observations of Ayse, and exchange thoughts about her learning, in the course of normal teaching. We met together, when we could, outside lessons to share our emerging ideas and questions. It was also valuable to be part of a wider research group carrying out similar work, so that we had an opportunity, from time to time, to think and speculate aloud with like-minded colleagues.

I kept a journal in which I recorded ongoing reflections and hypotheses about Ayse's learning and about our work in partnership. I found keeping a journal was a powerful tool for reflection. The act of stopping to think and write helped me to capture my own impressions and responses and to make sense of what might have been going on for Ayse. It was a challenging process, too, in terms of making time at the end of busy and demanding days to sit down and put pen to paper; and also in terms of forcing me to think through exchanges and classroom incidents that might otherwise have gone unnoticed. I'm an experiential learner and tend to apply learning enthusiastically to new situations without necessarily dwelling on reflection or abstracting from my thinking! The 'innovative thinking' framework prompted me to speculate on my responses more systematically and to extend and confront my own first impressions and instant judgements.

Getting to know Ayse

In my role as a support teacher, I arranged to visit Ayse and her parents at home, with an interpreter. I was invited to return, and did so on two further occasions. I also arranged to shadow Ayse for a day in order to try to gain a better understanding of what a day's learning experiences might be like for her. Both these activities proved to be very influential in beginning to change our perceptions of Ayse herself, and our concerns about her learning. Through the home visits, I learned that Ayse, the oldest child of the family, spent much of her time outside school helping with the care of new-born twins. This information revealed Ayse in a different light: not as a pupil needing help, but as a competent, independent person, entrusted with, and capable of carrying out, significant domestic responsibilities. It also enabled us to raise new questions about the connection between her external family responsibilities and her responses to school learning. How did these responsibilities affect her priorities? How did they affect her intellectual *availability* for engaging with the school curriculum?

As a result of the home visits, my relationship with Ayse also subtly changed. Ayse began to seek me out, to talk much more freely about herself and her experiences than she had done previously. I wondered if my visits home had somehow made the link between home and school more concrete, so that she began to feel a stronger sense of being known, of belonging. I began to reflect on this aspect of her school experience and its relationship with our perception of her seeming disconnection from academic work. I also shared with Lesley, and with the research group, my worries that I might be fostering a dependence on my personal input and interest that I might not be able to sustain (we do not always stay in the same school, or even stay working with the same teachers and pupils in one school, for extended periods).

In the context of this new intimacy, Ayse confided in me, during a group reading lesson, that her absence the previous day had been due to a dramatic incident at home. Her little brother had been taken ill, and it was she (the oldest and most responsible child) who had called the ambulance. An ambulance had been successfully summoned and her brother was now recovering. The sheer excitement of the story meant that it needed to be recounted in detail; I suggested to Ayse, too, that she might write it down. The resulting story captured much of the drama, suspense and emotion of her oral account; Lesley and I also noted that it was the most extended, and expressive, piece of writing she had produced so far (see Figure 9.1).

My day shadowing Ayse was also a salutary experience. As noted in Chapter 3, I found myself feeling quite confused by the demands and fragmented nature of the school day. It made me realise just how much effort is required of pupils to be ready to engage with the content of each lesson; and how much more difficult it must be to

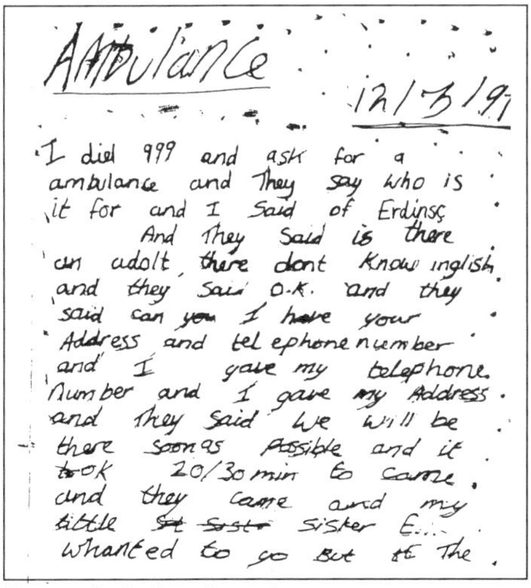
Ambulance 12/3/97

I did 999 and ask for a ambulance and they say who is it for and I said of Erdinsç And they said is there an adolt there dont know inglish and they said O.K. and they said can you I have your Address and telephone number and I gave my telephone Number and I gave my Address. and they said We will be there soon as possible and it took 20/30 min to came. and they came and my little ~~St~~ ~~Sist~~ Sister E... whanted to go but the

Figure 9.1 Ayse's written account

make that effort, if you are working in a language in which you are not fully fluent and confident. Of course, at one level I knew this already; yet that knowledge did not surface in my awareness, when we were worrying initially about Ayse's seeming lack of involvement in the curriculum. It was not a feature of the situation that we had thought to focus upon, or whose implications we had thought to pursue at a practical level.

These experiences, together with our ongoing observations, helped to us to explore our assumptions and begin to modify our view of Ayse. Our thoughts were still very tentative, though, at this stage. I wrote in my journal:

> Lesley has wondered if Ayse's frightened of really connecting with school and tasks or if it's all too big, overwhelming, alien. I don't know if that's the case. All I know is that I'm aware of working with a pupil who, while not alienated from school in many ways, and keen to be getting on, to be approved of, to be seen and supported, is not, generally, engaged with tasks. I don't know if that's because of something I/we/the school is doing or because of something that Ayse herself is doing/not doing . . . because she doesn't see the need or relevance.

Further experience helped us to decide which of our emerging ideas and hypotheses were worth pursuing. For instance, we rejected the idea that Ayse was afraid of something in the schooling process when our first, tentative attempts at nudging Ayse into greater involvement met with encouraging success. On this occasion, at the start of a topic on 'Free Willy', we arranged a home group/expert group exercise using information texts on whales. Pupils in each expert group had to research a particular aspect of information about whales (e.g. habitat, food, social behaviour), and then re-form into home groups, each member reporting the information that they had researched to the members of their group. They were also asked to carry out some research homework and Ayse brought in a detail from a story about whales.

Throughout this process, I had a strong sense of getting to know Ayse more fully, of her becoming more than a pupil who appeared to be struggling with aspects of the curriculum. As I tried to understand the complexities associated with Ayse's learning, so she seemed to emerge as an increasingly three-dimensional person, and this in turn meant that my relationship with her was richer and more real. I found it impossible then to be satisfied with any kind of limiting definition or label of her as a learner.

Reframing our initial perceptions

As we explored the significance of the new information available to us, the five questioning moves provided a framework for our discussion and encouraged us to challenge our own and each other's conclusions. Some of the questions that we found ourselves asking are summarised in Figure 9.2. The contradicting move was particularly powerful in helping us to search out plausible alternative readings of our initial assessment of Ayse's behaviour. Did she *see herself* as lacking involvement? Was she engaged with learning to the extent that she chose, or felt able, to be at that time? Did she have an agenda of her own – responsibilities at home, establishing her identity as a member of a small ethnic group within her class – which was more of a priority for her? Was it practically possible for her to engage meaningfully with activities? Was enough being done to activate her desire to learn?

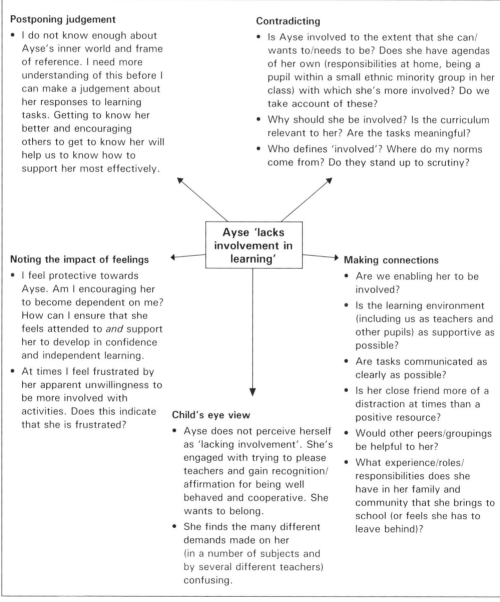

Postponing judgement

- I do not know enough about Ayse's inner world and frame of reference. I need more understanding of this before I can make a judgement about her responses to learning tasks. Getting to know her better and encouraging others to get to know her will help us to know how to support her most effectively.

Contradicting

- Is Ayse involved to the extent that she can/wants to/needs to be? Does she have agendas of her own (responsibilities at home, being a pupil within a small ethnic minority group in her class) with which she's more involved? Do we take account of these?
- Why should she be involved? Is the curriculum relevant to her? Are the tasks meaningful?
- Who defines 'involved'? Where do my norms come from? Do they stand up to scrutiny?

Ayse 'lacks involvement in learning'

Noting the impact of feelings

- I feel protective towards Ayse. Am I encouraging her to become dependent on me? How can I ensure that she feels attended to *and* support her to develop in confidence and independent learning.
- At times I feel frustrated by her apparent unwillingness to be more involved with activities. Does this indicate that she is frustrated?

Child's eye view

- Ayse does not perceive herself as 'lacking involvement'. She's engaged with trying to please teachers and gain recognition/affirmation for being well behaved and cooperative. She wants to belong.
- She finds the many different demands made on her (in a number of subjects and by several different teachers) confusing.

Making connections

- Are we enabling her to be involved?
- Is the learning environment (including us as teachers and other pupils) as supportive as possible?
- Are tasks communicated as clearly as possible?
- Is her close friend more of a distraction at times than a positive resource?
- Would other peers/groupings be helpful to her?
- What experience/roles/responsibilities does she have in her family and community that she brings to school (or feels she has to leave behind)?

Figure 9.2 Questions about Ayse's learning

On the basis of what we had learnt so far, our provisional conclusion was that Ayse probably was involved as much as she wanted – or perhaps felt able and safe – to be at this time. She was fully involved in those areas of school life where she knew she could be successful, where she was noticed and appreciated through helping with classroom tasks, and being a polite, friendly pupil. To engage academically, however, was far more risky. What we had seen initially as lack of involvement, we now saw more as a sense of uncertainty about her own place, academically, within the group. She was uncertain, we felt, that she belonged academically, was not confident about what she had to contribute. If so, then we had to try to give her a stronger sense of her place, value and capacity to make a contribution. The onus was on us to try to create the kinds of conditions where she would feel as comfortable and secure, and as expectant and desirous of success, as she already did in those areas where she currently involved herself fully.

Planning to involve Ayse

The work of Jim Cummins (1996) reminded us that this was not a task which related solely to the conditions surrounding the teaching–learning relationship between Ayse and ourselves. We also needed to think about how to create conditions that would help to establish more firmly Ayse's central and equal place, as a learner with a contribution to make, within the overall class group. Cummins argues that one of the most important things a teacher can do in order to promote academic interest and mastery is to 'organise the classroom as a learning community where everyone's voice can be heard. When students feel strong respect and affirmation from their teachers and peers, it generates a powerful sense of belonging to the classroom learning community and motivation to participate fully in the society beyond' (Cummins 1996: 91). It seemed to us that this was a particularly important consideration in our planning for including Ayse in the learning process and, indeed, in establishing the context for engaging all pupils in a multilingual, mixed-ability setting.

In Ayse's class, not only were the dynamics of all school-based groups present but also the added dimension of differences in cultural and educational background and languages of the pupils, with the inevitable potential for prejudice and racism. In our work, we needed to think about how to create a stronger sense of community, an issue highlighted by Watts and Bentley (1989: 161) who note that 'In any environment, the very act of learning is an emotional affair'. Given that learning is inherently risky, if pupils are to engage actively in making sense of information and ideas, if they are to express and explore personal views, they need to feel safe and supported. Teachers are responsible for creating an atmosphere in which such interactions can take place, and we do this as much by the way in which we act as by what we say. Actions that enable youngsters to feel positive about themselves aid the process of cognitive change. From evidence amassed by Watts and Bentley, it seems that pupils are keen interpreters of teacher behaviour and this is borne out in my own experience. Bilingual pupils, in particular, have made it clear to me that they are looking for welcoming, positive and encouraging attitudes on the part of teachers whether or not a common language is shared!

We explored ways of enhancing conditions for Ayse's academic involvement, through our work with the whole class. We worked together to devise a unit of work on visual literacy based around the video 'Free Willy', taking as a starting point Ayse's need to be drawn into curriculum activities, to extend her learning and enable her to feel empowered to make a contribution to listening, speaking, reading and writing tasks. Our intention was to structure the activities in such a way that Ayse could not fail to take an active learning role, focusing on the tasks set, contributing to discussion and demonstrating her understanding, ideas and opinions. Key features of our planning included the visual stimulus – a visual narrative text in easily accessible form, collaborative group work and support through talk and scaffolded reading and writing tasks, based on the EXIT model (Extending Interaction with Text) of interacting with texts (Wray and Lewis 1997). We aimed to provide multi-dimensional support – sensory, relational/interpersonal and structural – to enhance the possibility of real involvement. A summary of the tasks devised and the in-built support strategies adopted is shown in Figure 9.3.

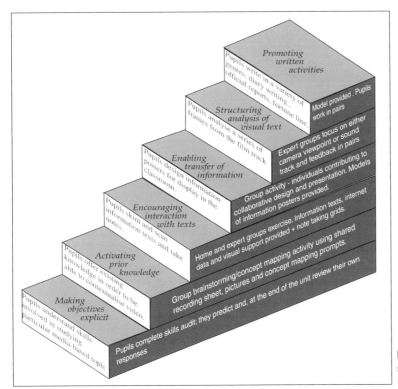

Figure 9.3 In-built support strategies (LcaS 1999)

It is tempting to see the unit as a metaphor for freeing Ayse herself from limits on learning and self-expression! As the work developed, we were able to observe the response of Ayse and the rest of the group, and to review and refine our strategies in the light of their responses. Examples of activities and of Ayse's written work are shown in Figure 9.4, including the fortune line technique (also discussed in Chapter 7) which encouraged pupils, working in pairs, to think carefully about the experiences of the main character and to discuss and plot these along two axes. The task was conceptually demanding without depending upon extended written evidence. I noted in my journal that Ayse 'seemed somehow in control of the material and the process'.

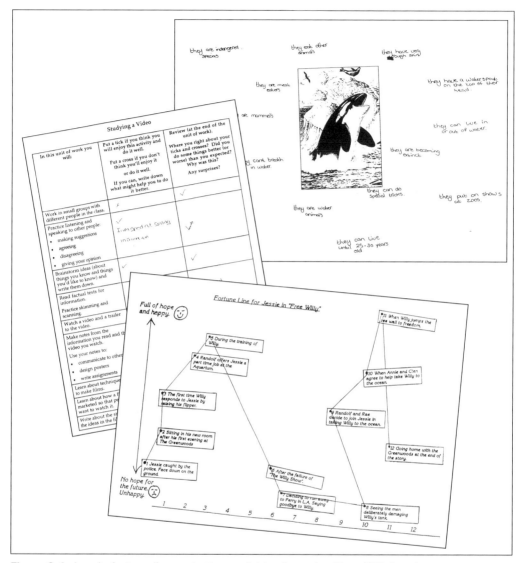

Figure 9.4 Ayse's fortune line and other activities from the 'Free Willy' project

As the unit of work progressed, one thing became clear to both of us. Anything we did that benefited Ayse, benefited *all* the pupils, including the most academically successful pupils. During the 'Free Willy' unit we found that the model and prompt sheet for a diary, to be written by the main character's foster mother, broadened the possible responses for all the pupils. Lead sentences devised to support Ayse's responses were not needed by many pupils, but having access to them suggested emotional responses pupils had not considered. Even higher achievers were tending to concentrate on the character's anger at the 'bad behaviour' of the newly arrived foster son. Prompt phrases such as 'I understand why he's being like this, but . . .' elicited sophisticated and empathetic evaluations of the foster child's past that were, in the hands of some pupils, genuinely moving. The use of teacher modelling was intended to get Ayse started on a few simple sentences. What we had not realised was that our adult view of the character's situation had crept into these prompts and acted as triggers of a quite different sort for other pupils.

Other ideas and strategies

In addition to planning for Ayse's inclusion at the level of the whole class we worked at acknowledging her more fully as an individual in our one-to-one interactions, recognising that within a large and complex secondary school there is the possibility of pupils becoming or feeling lost or invisible. Following the successful invitation to write about her personal experience calling the ambulance, I invited Ayse, along with a group of her peers, to express her thoughts and feelings in a confidential journal, to which Ayse responded enthusiastically 'I've got lots to write about'. I replied in writing, enabling Ayse to enjoy some personal 'conversations' and me to keep the child's eye view firmly in mind.

I explored too the possibility of including Ayse in the mentoring system established in the school and of pairing her with an older student for support with her reading. The day spent shadowing drew attention to the pressures presented by the school day, particularly for bilingual pupils, and I wondered if a worthwhile way of adapting the existing system might be to pair Year 7 pupils up with an older pupil, possibly one who speaks the same first language. This suggestion needed to be explored with colleagues in the learning support department who organised the mentoring system.

The day spent shadowing also set me thinking about what might be done at whole-school level to further develop opportunities for enhancing Ayse's, and others', involvement in the curriculum. Experiencing a series of lessons from a pupil's perspective made me realise how things might be made less fragmented and confusing if there were more shared systems in place relating to classroom routines and teacher expectations, and if teachers had more opportunity to share with one another perspectives on pupils and the approaches they use.

Thinking about the kinds of conditions that might support and foster Ayse's participation and learning thus led us to undertake developments, and identify possibilities for refining practice, not just at an individual level but at whole-class and whole-school level. We saw how pupils who appear to be struggling to access the curriculum can represent the litmus test of teaching and learning activities. If Ayse and others are not engaging with the tasks set, this indicates that we need to think about how the tasks might be reframed or presented differently. Our experience confirms an idea proposed by Ainscow (1999: 8) that pupils experiencing difficulties can be the 'hidden voices', the catalyst for new thinking and learning that can help to enhance learning opportunities for all.

Working with Ayse's class, and beyond – Lesley's story

Using the five questioning moves was powerful and productive, but it was made even more effective by the fact that Penny and I were working in partnership. Many teachers work in pairs or teams to plan or evaluate what they do in the classroom, and many speak of the advantages of collaboration. We felt these advantages were brought very sharply into focus when we worked with Ayse's class.

We were anxious to break away from the limiting features of the traditional demarcations between class teacher and support teacher. We planned the work together and, whilst accepting that Penny would have a closer focus on Ayse, we tried to work as a team in the classroom. We took various decisions about how we would operate so as to establish the idea that there were two teachers, rather than a 'real' teacher and a 'helper'. The huge benefits of such a teaching partnership are many, but the shared discussion and, most importantly, the shared progress through the moves are relevant here.

Initially it was very important to have the opportunity to simply observe Ayse. The partnership gave us both the opportunity to do this and to discuss what we saw in different circumstances. Even at this early stage we were challenging assumptions and modifying our view of Ayse. Once we began to use the moves as a framework for discussion, the partnership became even more valuable. We felt that this way of working had advantages for all pupils, not just those who were the focus of the original project.

As with any good idea it rapidly became part of our day-to-day working and often one or two of the moves, sometimes all five, would have particular relevance to a new teaching and learning situation. In the remainder of the chapter, I outline some ways in which the moves, and other ideas arising from our partnership work with Ayse's class, were applied in quite different situations.

Understanding Jodie

Disruptive behaviour is something all teachers have to contend with and, certainly in the later stages of the secondary school, can engender a level of panic in a teacher preparing a class for GCSE examinations. When valuable time for new learning and revision seems to be taken up by one badly behaved individual, teachers often feel that they must make choices between that disruptive pupil and the majority of the class. The teacher's irritation with the disruptive pupil becomes more marked, the pupil responds with aggression, or one of the many ways open to a single pupil to sabotage a lesson, and a vicious circle develops. As a head of department I have experienced that feeling of panic, and I have had to support other staff who have reached the end of their tether with a particular pupil.

Contradicting has been a particularly powerful move in one such case. 'This child is doing everything to sabotage my lesson' is the obvious interpretation of disruptive behaviour. If one tries out the idea of 'This child would very much like to be part of this lesson and a range of factors may be making her feel excluded from it', it is at least possible to move away from those bleak choices described above: either the disruptive pupil, or the majority of the class, must suffer.

With Jodie, a disaffected Year 10 pupil, I tried out this idea. It was difficult to imagine how she could wish to be part of the lesson when it seemed that every lesson was a carefully planned campaign on Jodie's part to ruin the atmosphere, goad me into losing my temper and, if possible, prompt me to send her out of the lesson. I knew that Jodie was intelligent and, in some circumstances, such as speaking and listening activities, she could be perceptive and articulate. She certainly understood the consequences of leaving school without any qualification in English.

At this point I felt more information was required. I talked to the head of year and discovered that Jodie was with foster parents after a clear and painful rejection by her mother. This had happened in Year 9, just before I first met Jodie in a new Year 10 GCSE class. This might explain why Jodie's behaviour was so negative and disruptive, but I felt no nearer to finding a way to work together. The next step was a combination of finding more information and seeing things from Jodie's point of view. The additional information came from Jodie. I asked her what career she hoped to take up. Jodie was quite certain she wanted to be a nursery nurse. Talking about her experiences with younger children in the foster family, and the baby-sitting she did for a number of the foster parents' friends, she became animated and enthusiastic. The surly, aggressive front she exhibited in lessons disappeared.

I offered Jodie a bag of picture story books I had collected over several years and said she was welcome to borrow any of them for her baby-sitting sessions. She asked if she could read them during the next English lesson. She read quietly and at the end of the lesson asked to borrow one book. She returned after a weekend to report on the success of the book with her charges. I suggested she might make a picture book of her own and we talked about some ideas. She worked on this for two weeks. I was grateful for the respite from her disruptive behaviour, but was uneasy on two counts.

Jodie might be behaving, but she was doing nothing towards her preparations for GCSE. Of more immediate concern was what she would do when her book was finished. I made a tentative suggestion that, with a commentary on how she set about making it, the book could be submitted as a piece of coursework under 'personal or imaginative writing'. Her reaction was lukewarm to say the least. What really gave me pause was the accusation from Jodie that I 'always had to spoil things'.

I tried using the moves that evening aware that what would happen the next day was crucial. If I could preserve the fragile goodwill between us, progress might be possible. If not, things might actually be worse than before because Jodie would feel I had let her down in some way. Seeing things from Jodie's point of view seemed key to this situation, and I could only guess at her reasons for reacting so strongly against anything to do with the GCSE course.

I had often come across pupils who behaved badly to divert attention away from their poor reading or writing skills, but Jodie was not in this category. She could have been in the top quarter of the class with very little effort. The contradicting move led me to question this. I was assuming she had an accurate picture of her own abilities. I was also assuming she understood what standard would be required of her at GCSE. The one thing I did not have time to do at this point was to postpone judgement. The thought of the 'old' Jodie back in lessons gave the situation urgency.

I went to find Jodie before our next lesson and, taking what felt like a very precarious chance, I showed her the folder of a pupil from a previous year who had achieved the grade Jodie needed to get onto a Nursery Nursing course. I asked if she could do work of that standard and she said, somewhat contemptuously, that she could *if she wanted to*. The next obvious question was 'Why don't you want to?' but I didn't get a chance to ask it. Jodie suggested I should 'get off her back' and she was gone. My amazement was total when, at the beginning of the next lesson, she came to my desk and said 'What's this commentary thing you want me to write?' I explained and she returned to her desk and worked on it for the rest of the lesson.

Jodie, gradually and grudgingly, began to take an interest in the lessons. The picture book and commentary were completed and I told her it was of a C grade standard. On the next piece of work she argued it was 'at least a B', and she was right.

The point of this example is that using the moves took things further than we might otherwise have gone. It would have been easy to stick at the point at which I found out about the rejection by her mother. This event may well have been the root of her aggressive behaviour, indeed this aggression did not disappear during the time I knew her. The real problem in English was her assumption that she was doomed to failure. What made a difference was the realisation that she could succeed.

Using an individual as a focus for reflection

Teaching my A level English class was another situation in which the moves and the work done with Ayse's class became relevant. A group of eleven Year 12 pupils were preparing for an examination in which they would have one hour to construct an essay on the play *Major Barbara* by George Bernard Shaw. Like many of Shaw's plays this piece is a dramatised debate about a variety of moral issues. In this case a rich arms dealer challenges the morality of his Salvation Army officer daughter. Once we had read the play, I began our exploration of the text with a series of symmetrical charts in which the beliefs of one character were set against the beliefs of another. What should have been lively classroom talk with a group of interested, articulate students turned out to be halting and uncertain. Of most concern to me was a rapid gathering of negative feeling about the text that would, I knew, make in-depth study very difficult. At the end of that lesson I asked the class if they could explain why they were making such heavy weather of this text. They had cheerfully tackled Shakespeare and Chaucer, so the language of the text should not have been a problem. They had studied and, they all agreed, enjoyed a novel, *Moon Tiger*, by Penelope Lively with a very complicated, non-linear narrative structure. *Major Barbara* was a simple chronological sequence of events by comparison. The students seemed unable to say any more than it was 'hard', and more worryingly, a few were saying it was 'boring'.

For the next lesson I wrote out summaries of the views expressed by five or six characters in the play. I gave them to the students in a chart and asked them to find passages in the play to match the summaries. The students completed the task, but it became a fairly pointless searching for key words. The prevailing gloom deepened.

At the same time as this work was going on, Penny and I were developing the 'Free Willy' unit with Ayse's class. What would happen, I asked myself, if I 'borrowed' one of the principles we were using with Ayse and applied it in another learning situation? With 'Free Willy' our planning was driven by consideration of the member of the group who was least equipped to tackle the work. I tried to identify which of the A level students was having most difficulty and realised it was the majority of the class. This did not help much, but it did make me realise that one member of the group *was* engaging with the text and seemed to see the point of it. This student, Alicia, was the daughter of an evangelical minister, and it struck me that she was unusual in that matters of faith and morality were part of her day-to-day life. She attended church regularly, and their house was also the focal point of their small community, so she would have heard formal and informal discussion of this kind.

Making these connections with Alicia's out-of-school experience helped to suggest how I might alter my approach. Whereas I had been presenting the play as a debate, I thought of ways of looking at the play as an examination of faith and loss of faith. Because the 'Free Willy' work was so fresh in my mind I tried making a fortune line of the progress of the main character Barbara. Instead of 'happy and secure'/'unhappy and insecure' on the vertical axis I tried 'certainty' and 'doubt'. I showed the fortune line idea to the group and invited them to select the key moments for consideration. Working in groups of three or four, they set about the task and I was delighted to note that voices were raised in argument within ten minutes. Copies of the play were being searched for evidence and even my despised charts of opposing views were being cited to support the selection of significant moments.

The experience provided an interesting variation on the theme that focusing on one individual can provide insights and lead to developments of practice from which all can benefit. In this case, it was the student who stood out by virtue of experiencing most *success* with the work who was the catalyst for developments that assisted the learning of the whole group. The students wrote essays about Barbara's journey with a very pleasing degree of confidence. We moved on to a new text after that, but we returned to *Major Barbara* for revision before the final exam. The students groaned as we began this work, but one told me cheerfully 'It's a lot shorter than *Measure for Measure* (the other play to be examined) and if you think about that fortune thingy you've got it all in your head!'

Engaging with different professional values

Away from school, I was asked by the local University Department of Education to work with the Licensed Teachers Group. The members of this group were all working as unqualified teachers, and had been released for one day per week for a year to gain qualified teacher status on a licensed teachers scheme. I had three one-hour sessions in which to investigate the way in which talk is central to the learning process. In the first session I showed the group a 'jig-saw' activity from our 'Free Willy' unit and explained the thinking that had gone into the work. I suggested that the students should think of some area of their own subject that might be explored through a jig-saw activity and asked them to explain to a partner how they would use it and how it might further pupil learning. One pair were obviously unhappy. Such 'games' might be appropriate in English, but they taught other subjects and in their experience the best results came from making sure the pupils listened. Talking was a disruption.

Over coffee at the end of the first session these two students were keen to explain their views and backed up what they said with examples from their own experience of teaching and their own educations. They were very much in my mind as I prepared for the second session and from the conversation I began to make connections. Many products of very formal educations, as these two students both were, are successful in examinations and go on to be high achievers. They look back to their classrooms in which teacher talk and pupil silence were the rule and conclude that since the system worked for them it will work for all. Both students now worked in schools where success in the classroom was gauged by the unbroken peace prevailing in it. Add to this the slightly uncomfortable position these two students experienced as unqualified teachers, and, looking at the issue through their eyes, I could see that it would take considerable courage on their part to risk their hard-earned control with 'games'. I could provide research evidence as to the value of talk but, in their eyes, they were being successful in promoting learning.

When thinking through this problem I came back to the work we had done with Ayse and her class. If we wished to be truly inclusive we had to consider the work from the point of view of the person least able to tackle the work. These two teachers were the least able to tackle the work because of the way in which circumstances had collided, producing a very fixed view about the place of talk. It occurred to me that I would get nowhere by talking about classroom situations. What I needed to do was to show them how talk could aid *their own learning*. I remembered an INSET session I had attended about working with bilingual pupils. A Turkish teacher conducted a lesson in Turkish and we had to make some sense of what was happening. It was an example of 'showing' being much more powerful than 'telling'. What I needed was something of similar power to show how talk works in the learning process.

For the next session I prepared the short story *The Flowers* by Alice Walker. Working in groups, the teachers read the opening section and the last line, and then tried to work out what would happen in the missing paragraph. After ten minutes, I gave them the missing paragraph on a separate sheet and waited for the stunned hush to settle on them as I knew it would, having used this story with students before. Then I asked them to go back and analyse how they had constructed their reading of the story. What did they know from the outset and what did they learn from others in the group? What began to emerge, in the discussion that ensued, was the complex picture of how meaning was made as a joint enterprise.

I have to say the two teachers who had been so resistant to the idea of talk in their own classroom were not suddenly converted. They were, however, more willing to try out some ideas I showed to the group and take them back to their own classrooms. I was not with them long enough to know if it really made a difference in the long term.

Conclusion: advantages for the teacher

In our partnership work with Ayse's class, our main concern was clearly the way in which using the moves benefited the pupils and furthered their learning. However, we felt there were also many benefits for teachers. The first, for us, was the enormous satisfaction of seeing Ayse's development in the months, now years, following the project. Ayse could so easily have been written off as a child with several different 'problems' and therefore unable to make significant progress in any aspect of her schooling. The fact that she was such a pleasant and well-behaved pupil probably made this more rather than less likely. To see the first signs of her engagement with the work, the first tentative contributions to discussion, was all very rewarding.

Using the moves also adds to a teacher's sense of empowerment. The moves do describe many of the things teachers do all the time, but learning to use them in a systematic yet flexible way has many advantages. It gives one permission to stop and think. Postponing judgement builds in this space and removes some of the pressure felt in day-to-day work.

Another important aspect of this empowerment is that, having the moves central to your thinking about pupils and learning situations helps you to avoid depressing 'dead ends'. By dead end, I mean those situations in which a teacher feels powerless, in which the idea of making a difference simply seems impossible. Entries in support registers listing a child's multiple difficulties can constitute a dead end. Another dead end can happen when we hear about a pupil's history – stories of neglect, abuse and prolonged misery. In the case of some refugee children, we know they have suffered in ways we can hardly imagine. We watch such children struggle to fit themselves into our neat and well-ordered learning environments and we can only guess at what the world looks like from inside their head. The dead end is in the assumption that there is nothing we can do. In such circumstances the teacher may be forgiven for thinking that inclusion is a nice idea, but not an option in this case.

All too often the way out of such a dead end is to look to the specialist learning and language support teacher. The problem with this is that even the most generous provision will not allow for the support teacher to withdraw or support the child all the time. When the child is back in the classroom, or has to function in the classroom without the support teacher, the problems can be exacerbated. The child has missed what the rest of the class are doing (in the case of withdrawal), or become dependent on the support teacher (in the case of in-class support). The class teacher feels even less able to make a difference. Using the moves and, wherever possible, using them to plan in partnership, gives teachers a way of making a start. By using moves such as 'looking from the child's point of view' and 'contradicting', the teachers begin to burrow under and squirm round the dead end, rather than being blocked by it.

One element of the stress suffered by teachers is, I would suggest, the feeling of helplessness and lack of control engendered by these dead ends. I am suggesting that having the moves as part of their repertoire of strategies will help teachers to reclaim control in potentially stressful situations.

PART FOUR

CHAPTER 10

Innovative thinking and school development

The two accounts of classroom work in Part Three illustrate the kinds of developments in thinking and practice that can be brought about when teachers use the framework for innovative thinking to support their own processes of reflective analysis of classroom experience. In both cases, the teachers chose to pursue possibilities for enhancing participation and learning that necessarily entailed considerable development work. The accounts were chosen in order to illustrate the *scope* that exists for enhancing learning through the approach to classroom analysis presented here.

However, as Lesley's contribution in the previous chapter illustrates, it is also possible to use innovative thinking in a way that is not enormously time consuming, and can readily be accommodated within the pressures and constraints under which teachers ordinarily work. In the Introduction, I suggested that the framework for innovative thinking is intended to support teachers in using as productively as possible whatever time that they *do* have available for reviewing and reflecting on their teaching. Throughout the book I have sought to emphasise that significant developments in thinking, which can have an important impact on practice, can be brought about in a very short space of time, even walking down a corridor, or during a brief exchange with another member of staff, travelling home or making a cup of coffee. Experience also suggests that teachers are more ready to invest time in this aspect of their work, if they expect worthwhile insights to come out of it and if they can see that it does benefit children.

Yet it is also the case that there is the potential to do so much more to improve children's participation and learning, if only teachers had more time and opportunity during the working day to review and reflect on their work. If teachers' powers of innovative thinking are not to remain continually under-used, we need to think of creative ways to make more space for reflection as an essential feature of teachers' professional work.

The time available for reflection depends, of course, not just upon individual circumstances and priorities but also upon what is done at an *institutional* level to validate and encourage individual teachers' reflective practice. Teachers are more likely to give such work priority in an institutional climate that explicitly recognises, values and nurtures reflective practice. It is important, therefore, that teachers with management responsibilities also accept the importance of maximising teachers' time for thinking through teaching, and the part that this can play in the overall school development agenda.

In this chapter, I explore the relationship between individual reflective practice and the wider processes of school development. I consider what might be done at management level to create a climate that supports and fosters innovative thinking, and to extend opportunities for individual and collaborative reflective practice as an integral part of schools' ongoing development work. With the Standards Fund now devolved to schools, there is real scope for visionary managers to utilise resources in ways which create opportunities for teachers to work together, to share in the analysis of classroom events and to help one another to generate, implement and evaluate new ideas in practice.

Linking individual reflective analysis with school development

The Enfield teachers' work illustrates how teachers' ongoing reflections upon classroom experience provide a continual stimulus for individual professional development and learning. As the practical examples in Part Three have shown, even when the analysis is focused on an individual child, it can raise questions about teaching and learning that are of relevance to teachers' work with children generally. It can also lead to developments in practice from which all pupils can benefit.

Teachers' ability to foster their own learning through reflective analysis of classroom experience is an essential and integral part of school development. Other development initiatives, however worthwhile in their own right, are no substitute for the ongoing, routine reflections which enable teachers to continually review and develop practice in the light of children's responses. Moreover, the potential for teachers to learn from one another's experience will be lost if no formal structures exist to enable teachers to exchange ideas and understandings. Two of the Enfield teachers, Karen and Gita, felt that there was so much more that could have been done to support Mohammed's learning (described in Chapter 7), if there had been more formally structured opportunities and encouragement for teachers to share their experiences of what had been found to make a difference in their own classrooms, and also their perceptions of what *might* make a difference if ideas were taken up and followed through within the curriculum more generally.

Since individual teachers' reflective practice often gives rise to ideas and possibilities for development that are beyond their own sphere of influence, structures and procedures need to be in place to ensure that these ideas can feed into the wider school development agenda. Teachers' *collective* power to make a difference to children's learning is potentially much greater than the sum of developments in thinking and practice brought about by individual teachers reflecting in individual classrooms. If development activities are organised in such a way as to facilitate the sharing of ideas between teachers, and across subject departments, and if there are channels of communication that encourage teachers to raise issues arising from their individual reflective practice as a possible focus for whole-school development work, teachers' individual reflective practice can become part of a powerful collective resource which can reciprocally support and stimulate work at an individual *and* at a whole-school level.

Some visionary managers have, for a number of years now, been attempting to develop their schools as reflective communities (e.g. James and Worrall 2000). A reflective community, in terms of the arguments presented in this book, would be a place where teachers' ability to think innovatively is explicitly prized; where it is recognised as one of the highest forms of professional expertise; where conditions are created in order that it can be actively nurtured; and where it is accorded a central role in schools' ongoing development work. Teachers in leadership roles can facilitate the development of such a climate, through decisions made regarding the use of directed hours, the use of INSET resources, approaches to staff development, and school development planning. Why, for instance, are after-school meetings so infrequently used for the detailed examination and discussion of teaching and learning? Could more of the time currently spent on joint planning be used for the reflective review of children's responses, as an essential prerequisite for further planning?

While there may be some leeway to use directed time differently, it is important also to acknowledge that, in the current context, development work in schools is largely being dictated by the external political agenda and by centrally imposed initiatives, requirements and targets. These appear, on the surface, to have little connection with the highly specific, fine-grained analyses of classroom experience exemplified in this book. In many cases, funds for INSET and development work are already stretched to the limits, supporting teachers in meeting these external demands, which also divert reserves of time and energy that otherwise might be available to support the reflective analysis of teaching. Some creative thought is needed, therefore, working with the reality of the current situation, to see how schools' responses to nationally defined priorities and initiatives might be developed in ways which *also* extend the time and opportunities available for teachers for careful, sustained reflection upon classroom experience.

Innovative thinking and current development initiatives

To explore this possibility more fully, I shall examine three current initiatives being promoted nationally, as part of the drive to raise achievement in schools. I shall consider the essential part that the reflective analysis of teaching can and should play in their implementation, and the opportunities that these initiatives present for teachers to support one another in reviewing and reflecting on their work.

Raising standards of literacy and numeracy

Development work in primary schools is currently focusing predominantly on literacy and numeracy (DfEE 1998a; 1999a). It is expected that most schools will follow the teaching objectives and approaches laid down in the nationally defined frameworks, although there is some uncertainty about how much discretion teachers have to deviate from the objectives and teaching strategies outlined. Any externally defined curriculum needs to be adapted, however, to the needs of particular classes, groups and individuals in different contexts. The processes of implementation of an externally prescribed curriculum programme necessarily involve teachers in making the new approaches meaningful in their own terms (Fullan 1982; 1991). The original ideas inevitably undergo change as teachers make sense of them in relation to their own existing understandings and experience, as they critically evaluate them in relation to their own values, and discover if and how they can work with them in a way that satisfies their own beliefs and aspirations for children's learning.

One key resource that teachers need to guide them in this development process is the feedback provided by children's responses to their teaching. Teachers need to spend time processing what happened, thinking about the nature of the learning that took place, exploring what they might have done differently, and using the insights to guide their future work. Indeed, this is not just an interim process. In the longer term, there will be a need to vary and revitalise the range of approaches currently being used in order to sustain the children's interest and foster their full engagement in literacy and numeracy learning. Teachers' ability to be creative in evolving practices in the light of experience will depend upon the extent to which they have taken control of the initiative and found ways of working with it that make sense in their own terms.

There are naturally occurring opportunities for teachers and other educators to engage together in this process of reflective analysis. Where a teaching assistant, support teacher or other adult is present, the second person can observe the children's engagement with the whole-class elements of the Literacy/Numeracy Hour in a more detached way than the teacher who is immersed in the interaction. A second pair of eyes will provide a valuable additional perspective, noticing things which the teacher may have missed, as well as providing important information about the activities and responses of the groups who were engaged in independent work, while the teacher was fully engaged with a particular group. Time to process the feedback from the lesson together will inevitably be limited, unless special arrangements can be made (through creative timetabling or the use of INSET resources) to free the two members of staff for a short period each week to review their work and plan how to build on their shared insights and understandings. Nevertheless, even a few words exchanged at the end of the session can be enough to stimulate new thinking and suggest possible adjustments or developments.

At secondary level, where the approach to improving literacy is less tightly defined (DfEE 1999b), there may be more scope for selecting strategies which nurture and facilitate opportunities for innovative thinking. The video supplied with the training materials represents literacy development as a whole-school initiative, potentially involving all subject areas. A menu of possibilities is provided, but there are no prescriptions for what schools should actually do. It is left up to each school to evolve its own set of strategies for literacy improvement. One possible approach, exemplified in an impressive extended video clip of a geography lesson, is for teachers in a particular subject area to explore together how to improve learning of their particular subject through a conscious focus on improving literacy.

The development of richly productive approaches to teaching and learning of the kind demonstrated in this geography lesson is not achieved simply by the care and thought that is put in at the planning stage. The feedback provided by pupils' responses is what enables materials, activities and classroom organisation to be progressively refined, and any necessary steps taken to encourage pupils to work productively together. Clearly, such ongoing development work will be greatly facilitated by time being made available (say through the use of INSET resources) for teachers to work together not just to plan but to evaluate their teaching, and if possible even have the opportunity to observe in one another's classrooms so that shared experience can provide the basis for mutual learning. The framework for classroom analysis proposed in this book could be used to support this process.

Data analysis and target setting

Another strand of government's drive to raise standards of achievement and improve schools' performance involves the use of 'evidence' to inform the processes of review and set targets for development. Anecdotal information suggests that, within the space of just a few years, the systems put in place for the overall monitoring of pupils' progress and achievement have, in some secondary schools, virtually taken over as the internal means by which the effectiveness of teaching is evaluated, and by which priority areas for development work are identified. Teacher reflection is harnessed to make sense of the numerical data emerging from these systems and generate appropriate responses, rather than being directed towards the ongoing, close analysis and interpretation of situations arising in classrooms.

Many teachers in my experience have considerable reservations about the new focus on data-monitoring systems and targets. Although they are committed to enhancing the participation and learning of the children in their classes through their own efforts, they feel less committed to targets generated on the basis of numerical data and from global comparisons made in relation to national averages. If targets are disconnected from the endeavour to understand children's responses to classroom experience, and to improve learning opportunities in the light of that understanding, they may more effectively serve the interests of politicians than those of children. Some teachers fear that, unless human concern and experience-grounded insight underpin these systems, the business of setting targets may prove to have been a diversion from the real task of making the curriculum accessible, meaningful and enabling for all children.

However, there is recognition, too, that data analysis can also be a powerful way of highlighting concerns and raising questions. These questions can then be pursued through classroom inquiry and the insights used to inform development work. In such cases, the data analysis serves to establish that there is indeed an issue to be addressed (for example, the relative achievement of particular minority ethnic groups) but leaves open the question of how the patterns identified in the data are to be explained, and what might be done about them. If, as a result of data analysis, funding is made available to support inquiry and development work, rooted in the analysis of classroom practice, the process of meeting targets can indeed connect up with teachers' commitments to enhancing participation and learning, while making available more officially sanctioned time to engage in reflective thinking about teaching and learning. Through such collective work, teachers will not just use their existing expertise, but *develop* their understandings of what makes a difference to how children respond and to what they learn. Such work can thus contribute to a growing body of knowledge about classroom processes that can be shared more widely with other teachers.

Teaching as a research-based profession

Extending the uses made of evidence to inform the development of practice is also a key theme of the Teacher Training Agency's recent initiative to encourage a view of teaching as a research-based profession. While there are differing interpretations among proponents of this view about what is meant by 'evidence' and by 'research' and about their relationship to practice, common to all is a concern about the lack of influence which educational research has traditionally had upon practice in schools. Explaining why the Teacher Training Agency has been promoting teaching as a research-based profession, Philippa Cordingley, the chief professional adviser for research, argues that research and evidence have a vital part to play in helping 'teachers do what they want to do most – help their pupils to achieve more' (Cordingley 1998). What is needed, she proposes, is 'a high quality body of research and evidence about what works in classrooms', plus mechanisms that involve teachers both in contributing to the development of a research agenda and in identifying the implications of research and evidence for classroom practice.

However, Cordingley also recognises that research outcomes cannot prescribe for practitioners what they should do in particular situations.

> (Reflective practitioners) are certainly interested in hard evidence about the relationship between teaching strategies and pupil outcomes, especially learning gain which they embrace with rigour where they can find it. But they understand too the complexity of teaching and learning in classrooms with multiple, complex, dynamically interacting variables and the need for reflection; for scrutiny of current practice which digs below the surface to make what may have become routine and implicit sufficiently explicit to allow re-evaluation in the light of new knowledge, strategies and ideas.   (Cordingley 1999: 1)

Cordingley is keen that the activity of interpreting evidence developed by others should be seen by teachers and managers as a high status activity that is central to reflective practice. The aim of developing teaching as a research-based profession is to encourage in teachers a thirst for interrogating evidence from research and other activities as a natural part of their efforts to raise standards (Cordingley 1999). This does not necessarily imply teachers themselves engaging in research, but certainly requires teachers to have a 'louder voice' in setting the agenda for research. It also raises challenging questions about the conditions which best facilitate teachers' access to research evidence, and the active use and interrogation of that evidence through reflective practice.

Knowledge-generating schools

A radical view of what needs to be done to bridge the traditional divide between research and practice is presented by David Hargreaves in his paper *Creative Professionalism* (1998). The vision that he presents is of knowledge-creating schools, where new knowledge is built out of the creative 'tinkering' that teachers naturally do in their classrooms. Tinkering, according to Hargreaves (drawing on the work of Huberman 1992), is the source of new knowledge, and the means by which the ideas of others come to be tried out, validated and translated or transposed into other contexts. For tinkering to be more than an individual affair, however, carried out by teachers in the privacy of their classrooms, schools need to be structured to create opportunities for teachers to talk to one another about their teaching. The means need to be found, and opportunities systematically created, for teachers to make explicit knowledge that otherwise would remain implicit, and for teachers' convictions about what works for them, or their hunches about what would make a difference to pupils' learning, to be shared and validated in such a way that other practitioners find them worthy of attention.

Hargreaves's account provides a useful analysis of the conditions and structures that enable schools to capitalise and build upon the knowledge generated by individual teachers in individual classrooms, while *also* being open to knowledge generated externally. Key characteristics of knowledge-generating schools include: 'the provision of regular opportunities for reflection, dialogue, enquiry and networking in relation to professional knowledge and practice, and a high commitment to continuing professional development' (Hargreaves 1998: 26). Hargreaves notes that some schools are already well on the way to developing such conditions. Indeed, under the influence of these ideas, one forward-thinking LEA committed to the idea has already drawn up plans about how to facilitate the validation and cross-fertilisation of practitioners' knowledge on an LEA-wide basis (Lincoln 1999).

The role of innovative thinking

As the notion of teaching as a research-based profession is taken up by policy-makers and begins to exert an influence in schools, it may help to energise and reaffirm belief in the essential creativity of teaching, and help to create a climate that legitimates once again a measure of teacher-led innovation, within an externally prescribed curriculum. This climate of legitimation may also extend to the use of INSET funds or other external funding to free teachers to engage in thinking about teaching in a variety of ways associated with the critical and creative use of evidence to inform their teaching. Moreover, if and when a shift takes place in the deployment of external research funding from universities to schools, significant new opportunities may be opened up for teachers to engage in collaborative inquiry as an integral part of their professional work.

Many teachers do, of course, already define their own approach to their teaching as one of continuous learning and aspire to the 'extended' professionalism, described by Lawrence Stenhouse (1975: 144) more than two decades ago in the following terms:

- The commitment to systematic questioning of one's own teaching as a basis for development;
- The commitment and the skills to study one's own teaching;
- The concern to question and to test theory in practice by the use of those skills.

The critique of traditional educational research which is currently influencing policy at central government level is by no means a new idea. Dissatisfactions over the ownership of educational research and the theory–practice divide were part of the rationale underlying the teacher-as-researcher movement and the action research tradition (e.g. Elliott 1991) which have developed and sustained considerable support among practitioners and academics, both nationally and internationally, through the Collaborative Action Research Network (CARN). However, it is only recently that central government has begun to involve itself in the debate and hence open up the possibility of significant research funding being made available to schools.

The framework for innovative thinking proposed in this book could provide an important source of support for such developments. If, as I have argued, the five questioning moves do simply make explicit interpretive strategies which many teachers already use spontaneously in making sense of what is happening in their classrooms, using them for the purposes of reflective practice or research would indeed be consistent with Hargreaves's vision of building strategies for 'knowledge creation' upon what teachers already do. The framework also offers an in-built set of criteria for validating the soundness of new ideas and theories emerging, through the interplay between the different moves, as Hargreaves suggests may need to happen (1998: 45):

> But is social scientific validation of professional knowledge by formal research always the best form of validation? There is no simple answer, but I suggest that once teachers have gained confidence in knowledge creation, they will explore new forms of knowledge validation ... Just as in law courts rules of evidence have evolved about the admissibility of certain kinds of evidence, the weight of evidence and the standard of proof, so educational practitioners might develop rules of evidence to apply to their own circumstances.

The innovative thinking framework also offers an interpretation of the processes whereby the ideas of others, obtained through access to colleagues' thinking and practices, or through published literature and research, can be incorporated into practitioners' thinking and practice. Each of the chapters on the various different moves provides detailed illustration of how externally derived ideas can inform and strengthen the insights generated, expanding on the range of possible meanings considered and challenging existing perceptions and understandings. In this process, practitioners are not merely receiving and trying out the ideas of others. As Cordingley (1998) describes, they are already engaged in their own ongoing process of reviewing and reflecting on their practice and their encounters with new ideas feed into that process.

The Enfield teachers' research also illustrates other ways in which ideas derived from external sources can be used to inform their development work. Penny and Lesley (Chapter 9) drew extensively on the work of the Exel project (Wray and Lewis 1997) to help them in building appropriate support strategies for Ayse into the scheme of work that they were planning. Penny also drew inspiration from work on interactive writing (Hall and Robinson 1994) in developing the use of an interactive journal, which provided a stimulus to Ayse's writing development, and has been extended as an approach used with whole classes in Year 7. The fortune line technique (referred to in chapters 7 and 9) was drawn from a book on creative approaches to assessment (White and Gunstone 1992).

In each case, it was the teachers' ongoing reflective analysis that enabled them to recognise the value and relevance of particular strategies to the needs of particular learners. They were carefully selected for use because they corresponded to the teachers' emerging theories about the *kinds* of development that might make a difference to children's learning. But it needed the teachers to make the connection, to recognise their potential and then to work out how to use the ideas in their particular curriculum context. All this required active, creative thinking on the part of the teachers; as did the process of refining and developing the ideas in the light of children's responses. Teachers do not always have to 'reinvent the wheel', but ideas drawn from literature and research can only ever be a *resource*, not a substitute for the reflective analysis of classroom experience. Research can provide a direction and a rationale for particular development work; or it can suggest particular ideas and strategies for pursuing the particular direction and rationale worked out by the teacher. But it is still up to the teacher to interpret its relevance and mode of application in a particular classroom, to review and evaluate its impact, and take steps to adjust and further develop the ideas in the light of experience.

Teacher expertise, innovative thinking and practitioner research

This third feature of the current scene is perhaps the one where there is likely to be most scope for extending teachers' opportunities for engaging in reflective analysis. Predicated upon an essentially respectful view of teacher competence and a creative view of teacher knowledge and expertise, it promises to increase resources available to schools to pursue teachers' own agendas for inquiry and reflection, as well as encouraging more active use of literature and research to inform the development of practice in schools.

A similarly respectful view of teachers' professional thinking and expertise does, I hope, come across in the approach to reflective analysis presented in this book. Teachers' responsibilities for reviewing their judgements and practices arise from the sheer complexity of the teacher's task: the unpredictability of children's learning, and the inevitable limitations of spontaneous judgements made under pressure in a busy classroom. It is teachers' knowledge, experience and expertise which enables them to probe more deeply into the meaning of classroom events and generate new insights which provide a basis for the development of practice. It is the most expert and experienced teachers, therefore, who are best placed to exploit their power to make a difference to children's learning.

Moreover, I have argued elsewhere (Hart 1995; 1996) that innovative thinking, as a process of professional learning, can be used in the context of practice or research. If more funds are made available to schools so that teachers can be directly involved in formulating and pursuing their own questions through research, the framework proposed in this book could provide a valuable resource in developing methodologies that extend and build upon teachers' own sophisticated reflective practices, rather than requiring teachers to make use of social science research methods which may be unfamiliar and, initially at least, deskilling.

In this chapter, I have explored some of the ways in which it might be possible to extend the time available for innovative thinking, by making legitimate use of funds allocated for specific development initiatives. The work of the Enfield teachers illustrates the benefits that could accrue if ways can be found to give more priority to this aspect of teachers' work. It also illustrates, by implication, the consequences for children's learning opportunities if we leave this important resource of teachers' thinking untapped. With the Standards Fund now devolved to schools, there is real scope for utilising resources in ways which give high profile to teachers' creativity and underline the important responsibilities towards children that are fulfilled through the process of thinking through teaching.

Finally, the discussion of this chapter would be too conservative, in its vision of possible futures, if consideration were not also given to the possibility that, at some future point, teachers' traditional conditions of work might undergo change; that policy-makers – recognising the importance of reflection – might decide that the most fruitful and enduring way to promote school development and enhance achievement might be to give teachers more time, within normal working hours, to review and reflect upon their teaching.

CHAPTER 11

Developing schools' capacity for inclusion

How schools interpret their responsibilities for providing support for children experiencing difficulties and choose to make use of additional funds is another area where there is considerable scope for extending teachers' opportunities for review and reflection on their teaching. If thinking through teaching is understood to be an important part of this task, then support systems can be specifically designed in such a way as to increase mainstream teachers' opportunities for reviewing and reflecting on their work.

The Enfield research was originally prompted by concerns about the impact upon bilingual pupils of the *Code of Practice on the Identification and Assessment of Special Educational Needs* (DfE 1994). Teachers in the Language and Curriculum Access Service were concerned about the assessment procedures leading to the placement of bilingual pupils on special needs registers; and also about the trends towards highly individualised forms of provision which could narrow learning opportunities for bilingual children (Hall 1996; Hart and Travers 1999). They were convinced that there was scope for developing a more inclusive approach to support for children experiencing difficulties, where the provision of support for individuals would become an integral part of the task of building a supportive and enabling learning environment for all pupils.

Their work therefore also affords a useful standpoint from which to take a fresh look, in this chapter, at the guidance provided by the *Code of Practice*, and at the proposals for revising the existing *Code*, in the light of the new government commitment to inclusion (DfEE 1997a; 1997b; 1998b). What would be the key characteristics of a genuinely inclusive approach to support? What is, or should be, the relationship between the systems of support that we set up in order to fulfil schools' responsibilities towards children experiencing difficulties and the everyday reflective practice which (I have argued) is a central part of all teachers' professional work? What changes need to be made to the existing *Code of Practice* if systems of support are to contribute actively to the task of building schools' capacity for inclusion?

Reviewing the existing code of practice

The existing *Code of Practice*, introduced in 1994, was designed to ensure that necessary steps were taken in schools to identify the needs of children whose learning was giving cause for concern and to provide appropriate support. The expectation was that, if appropriate support was provided by the school as soon as concerns arose, difficulties might in many cases be overcome and so those children would cease to require additional support. The *Code* proposes a five-stage process, with the first three stages being concerned with support that can be provided from within the schools' existing resources, and the fourth and fifth stages concerned with the production and implementation of a statement – at which point responsibility for ensuring that appropriate support is provided shifts from the school to the LEA.

The principles and procedures outlined in the *Code* do not have statutory force, but experience indicates that most schools have attempted to bring their existing systems of support in line with the *Code*'s recommendations. Surveys of practitioners' views, undertaken since the *Code* was introduced (e.g. Lewis *et al.* 1996), suggest that there is widespread support for the underlying principles. Nevertheless, considerable problems have also been experienced in attempting to develop systems of support along the recommended lines. Many schools report having found the procedures proposed unduly cumbersome and time consuming. Practitioners feel that too much time and energy is being spent on paperwork instead of providing practical support for teaching and learning in the classroom.

Acknowledging these concerns, the *Programme of Action* (DfEE 1998b: 14) proposes 'introducing a simplified SEN *Code of Practice* in 2000/2001 which ... focuses on preventative work, reduces bureaucracy and promotes effective school-based support and monitoring'. One key proposal is to reduce the three school-based stages to two, effectively abolishing the existing Stage 1, and replacing Stages 2 and 3 with 'support' and 'support plus'. The rationale for this change is explained as follows:

> Some children currently placed at stage 1 do not have special educational needs as defined by law. Whilst their progress needs to be carefully monitored, and there may need to be some differentiation of classroom work, they do not need provision which is 'additional to, or otherwise different' from that made generally available for children of the same age in local schools, such as an individual learning or support programme or special materials and equipment. We consider that the SEN Code of Practice should apply to children for whom there is clear expectation that they are likely to need help which is genuinely 'additional to, or otherwise different'. At present a child normally comes into this category only at stage 2 when he or she is given an IEP.   (DfEE 1998b: 16)

Advocates of this change argue that it will help to ensure that more children's needs are recognised and met within 'what is generally provided for all', while ensuring that those children who do need additional help receive the support to which they are entitled. My concerns are that it will further encourage the development of systems of support which are disconnected from, rather than integrally bound up with, the processes of reflective analysis of classroom experience. It may also discourage teachers from routinely questioning features of what is generally provided for all as a necessary and integral feature of their response to individuals perceived to be experiencing difficulties. I will examine each of these areas of concern in turn.

Building systems of support upon teachers' routine reflective practice

In the early chapters of the book, I explained in some detail why I believe that thinking through teaching is such an important part of all teachers' professional work. With the help of two examples, I argued that we have a particular responsibility to review and reflect upon our thinking and teaching when we find ourselves making judgements that reflect negatively on children's characteristics and abilities, or when children do not seem to be deriving as much benefit as we hope and expect from learning activities provided. I suggested that our ability to process classroom experience in such a way as to open up new insights and possibilities for practice is the means by which we not only fulfil these essential responsibilities, but also exploit our power to make a difference to children's learning.

It follows from these arguments that one of the most important ways in which additional funds can be used to support children experiencing difficulties is by making more time and opportunity available for teachers to engage in careful, reflective analysis focused on individual children. No matter how much mainstream teachers value and try to prioritise the review phase of their work, they necessarily take in far more information than they can process in the normal course of events. There are always more individual children whose responses demand urgent thought than it is possible to make the focus of sustained, reflective attention. Systems of support need to be organised, therefore, in such a way as to affirm, support and build on teachers' everyday reflective practice. It is mainstream teachers who have access to the information needed in order for judgements to be reviewed; it is they who every day can encounter the fresh evidence of children's engagement with classroom learning experience needed to generate new insights into what can be done to enhance learning within mainstream teaching.

Yet the existing *Code of Practice* makes no mention of the importance of generating support strategies through the sustained and continuing analysis of children's engagement with classroom learning activities. Indeed, from Stage 2, responsibility for the analysis of information about the child rests with the SENCO, who will inevitably have little, if any, direct knowledge of how individual children engage with learning experiences in the classroom. This encourages the use of off-the-shelf support strategies (Tod *et al.* 1998) based on predominately summative information. It disconnects support from active consideration of relationship between children's attainments, qualities and characteristics and the particular learning contexts and opportunities in which these abilities have been displayed and developed, and with the interpretive frameworks in terms of which they have been assessed. Additional help often comes in the form of a discrete package, administered to an individual child by a support assistant, disconnected from mainstream teachers' thinking about their teaching, and from the work being provided for the rest of the group.

The work of the Enfield research group demonstrates, in contrast, the very different form that additional support can take when the focus is the ongoing reflective analysis of classroom experience, and when teachers have the opportunity to explore ideas together and support one another in reviewing and developing classroom practice. Their alternative approach involves teachers, and other support staff, in analysing the information arising from day-to-day classroom interaction, translating new understandings immediately into strategies for action, implementing these strategies, and then reviewing their impact in the light of the feedback provided by children's responses. Their work highlights the opportunities for revising judgements and developing practices that will be missed, if we allow – indeed, encourage – the development of support systems which are not connected to and informed by teachers' everyday reflective practice. An entitlement to additional provision is no substitute for the more fundamental entitlements secured by mainstream teachers' ongoing reflections upon their work.

Reviewing what is generally provided for all

The Enfield research also illustrates the need to look closely at what is implied by the definition of 'support' put forward in the *Programme of Action*, as help which is genuinely 'additional to or otherwise different from what is generally provided for all'. To hold constant in our minds what is generally provided for all is to place an unnecessary, indeed untenable, limit on the scope of schools' possible responses to individual difficulties. Teachers need to be prepared to question and rethink what is generally provided for all children as a necessary and integral part of any response to individual difficulties, if systems of support are not to perpetuate unwittingly the circumstances that are creating the need for additional support in the first place.

In Chapter 8, for example, we saw how Asad's teachers chose to address Asad's perceived difficulties in negotiating relationships with other children, and his professed discomfort in working in particular groups. They saw this not as an isolated individual problem but as an issue that needed be addressed through carefully structured work with the whole class on feelings, relationships and respectful listening, as part of their curriculum for Personal, Social and Health Education. They also saw scope for addressing Asad's needs through adaptations made to the content of the whole-class geography topic, extending work on India and Britain to include Bangladesh, so that Asad had an opportunity to contribute his knowledge and expertise as a resource for the whole group. In addition, they reviewed the source materials and conceptual demands of tasks with which Asad had appeared to experience difficulty, and determined to look for more personal ways of enabling *all* children – not just Asad – to engage more successfully with historical ideas and concepts that were far removed from their own experience.

Their effort to understand the dynamics of Asad's engagement with classroom experiences helped them to see ways of intervening in those dynamics in order to encourage Asad's acceptance and positive involvement within the group, as well as enhancing his learning. Doing this required some systematic rethinking of what was currently being provided for all children, and a conscious commitment to making adjustments to their planning to take account of Asad's perceived needs. Moreover, they did not consider that, in the various different kinds of development work undertaken, they were subordinating other children's needs to those of Asad. On the contrary, Asad's difficulties helped to confirm and consolidate their sense of where their priorities lay for enhancing the learning of the whole group: particularly in the area of encouraging more productive group work and developing strategies that would assist the children to have more personal engagement with historical ideas.

Similarly, in Chapter 9, we saw how Ayse's teachers, concerned about her 'lack of involvement', were led to take a fresh look at the experiences currently being provided for all children, asking themselves about their relevance and appropriateness to Ayse. They used the outcomes of this review to guide their planning of a new unit of work for the whole class, ensuring that whatever support they thought that Ayse would need in order to engage fully in the sequence of activities and be successful was built into their planning. There was no need to provide something additional or different from what was generally provided for all, specifically for Ayse, because the unit of work had been planned taking Ayse's needs into account.

An approach that recognises the need to question and make adjustments to what is generally provided for all does not *exclude* the possibility that some additional or different provision for individuals might *also* be appropriate, as Ayse's story illustrates. Ayse's personal dialogue with Penny, for example, through the use of an interactive journal, appeared to have played a role in fostering Ayse's writing development. Strategies for supporting Ayse's learning were identified and pursued at a whole-class, whole-school *and* an individual level. What is important is to ensure that extra or different provision is not allowed to function as a substitute for the necessary process of rethinking and reconstruction of mainstream learning environments upon which children's curriculum entitlement depends.

As Tod (1999: 99) points out, notions of 'extra' and 'different' are *relative* to 'what is generally provided for all'. The most economic and effective strategy for teachers may be to make changes to what is currently provided for all, so that fewer children emerge who appear to require extra and different provision. Systems of support need to be organised in such a way that strategies for addressing difficulties can encompass possibilities for change and development at whole-class and, sometimes too, at whole-school level. Again, this is an area which receives no explicit mention in the existing *Code of Practice*. Although the *Code* does not explicitly state that an individual education plan (IEP) needs to be addressed through individualised *provision*, neither does it offer any suggestions that might actively encourage schools to consider the merits of generalised rather than individualised approaches. Some explicit reference needs to be made to the legitimacy, and indeed desirability, of such approaches, if schools are to be encouraged to develop systems of support which exploit more fully these wider possibilities.

Towards a more inclusive education system

This is an important principle to establish, if there is a genuine intention to encourage the development of a more inclusive education system. We need to consider carefully how we organise systems of support for children experiencing difficulties so that they can actively contribute to the task of building schools' capacity for inclusion. The white paper *Excellence in Schools* acknowledges that there are compelling educational, as well as moral and social, arguments in favour of inclusion (DfEE 1997a: 34) and significant funding has been made available for development work. Promoting inclusion is seen as an important part of building an inclusive society; and there is encouraging evidence that where schools are fostering an inclusive approach, this 'can reinforce a commitment to higher standards of achievement for all children' (DfEE 1998b: 23).

As the *Programme of Action* acknowledges, the notion of inclusion is open to different interpretations.

> The term can be used to mean many things, including the placement of pupils with SEN in mainstream schools; the participation of all pupils in the curriculum and social life of the school; the participation of all pupils in learning which leads to the highest possible levels of achievement; and the participation of young people in the full range of social experiences and opportunities once they have left school.   (DfEE 1998b: 23)

The statutory inclusion statement in the new National Curriculum orders (DfEE/QCA 1999) helpfully clarifies the meaning of inclusion in curricular, rather than just locational, terms. It means 'providing effective learning opportunities for all pupils'. Understood as a process, not a state, inclusion involves 'the progressive extension of the capacity of mainstream schools to provide for children with a wide range of needs' (DfEE 1998b).

The reality of the current situation is that there are many young people already within mainstream schools whose experience is one of disengagement and disaffection, and who appear to be deriving little benefit from the educational opportunities made available for them. Official figures show that record numbers of pupils are being excluded from schools for disciplinary reasons, and many commentators see the rise in exclusion rates as being directly linked, ironically, to developments in education intended to improve schools and raise standards (Hayden 1997; Ball 1993; Stirling 1996).

In the process of working towards a more inclusive education system, it is important not to overlook the exclusionary influences operating upon and within schools. These can often be very subtle, and indeed bound up with practices that are so taken for granted, or are generally assumed to have a positive impact, that we do not think to question them. Well-intentioned additional or different provision for individuals can be exclusionary in its effects, if it diverts attention away from the search for possibilities for enhancing learning *within* what is generally provided for all. Indeed, on the basis of the Enfield teachers' work, it might be argued that a genuinely inclusive approach is one which responds to perceived difficulties by asking *first* how we can adjust or develop what we are providing for all children so that those who are currently experiencing difficulties can be more effectively included, and enabled to learn, within the range of experiences provided for the whole class, without the need for additional support.

Enhancing individuals' sense of 'acknowledgement'

Nevertheless, there might be another way of making sense of the definition of 'support' in the *Programme of Action,* which *would* be consistent with the recognition that there is a need for the continual questioning and development of what is generally provided for all at the level of general curriculum experience. One key outcome of the Enfield teachers' research was the realisation that the process of paying sustained attention to individual children *in itself* subtly changed the dynamics of the situation, affecting their perceptions of individual children, how the children responded to them and how they responded to classroom learning experiences.

Although it seems obvious, once stated, it was not at all obvious at the time. Only in retrospect did people realise how faint and two-dimensional their perceptions of the children had been at the outset, even though they felt that they already knew a good deal about them and, in most cases, had formed a positive relationship with them. The studies brought a new quality to their perceptions and interactions by bringing about both a more appreciative, multi-faceted awareness of the individuality of the child on the teacher's part, and a perceptible blossoming on the part of the child who picked up on and responded to the teacher's sustained interest.

Searching for a word to represent this new sense of value and being valued, the teachers felt that the notion of acknowledgement discussed by Pye (1988) in relation to the 'invisible children' in schools that concerned him, most closely corresponded to what had clearly emerged as a common experience across all the case studies. Acknowledgement involves *two-way recognition*: on the part of teachers, it is a recognition of the interesting individuality and complexity of the child, which is *communicated to* the child; on the part of the child, it is an active awareness of and response to the sense of being recognised as an interesting, complex and unpredictable individual whom the teacher considers important and wants to continue to get to know.

Once the teachers had become aware of this new quality that had developed in their relationship with the children, it occurred to them that this might in fact be a precondition for the success of any other, specific strategies used to enhance children's learning. A heightened sense of acknowledgement might be what persuades the child to take up whatever enhanced learning opportunities are introduced, whether at an individual, whole-class or whole-school level. Without it, the most innovative, imaginative and potentially inclusive strategies for support might fail to have any significant effect. As Cummins argues:

> The interactions that take place between students and teachers and among students are more central to student success than any method for teaching literacy or science or math . . .When students' developing sense of self is affirmed and extended through their interactions with teachers, they are more likely to apply themselves to academic effort and participate actively in instruction.
>
> (Cummins 1996: 2).

However, a sense of acknowledgement on the part of the child is a product of genuine regard; it cannot be fabricated and communicated if it is not genuinely *felt* and experienced by the teacher. As the example of Emer and Costas shows, a necessary condition for the development of genuine acknowledgement between teacher and child is an openness that allows existing perceptions to be reconsidered. It requires a commitment on the part of teachers to searching out the reason and competence underlying the child's response, even when this is different from what the teacher expects or desires.

The kinds of thinking that these teachers were routinely using, with the support of the framework, to make sense of classroom events may thus have played an integral part in the development of this new quality. They provide an ever-present reminder to question spontaneous judgements, and probe the meaning of classroom events from a variety of different points of view. They may have helped teachers to develop and sustain over time a much more positive and optimistic perception of children's competence as individuals and as learners. In this way, they helped to create the conditions in which a stronger sense of mutual acknowledgement could evolve.

If the new quality in their relationships with individual children was indeed brought about by the extra time, interest and careful thought that they were able to give in a sustained way to the classroom responses of individual children, this provides a further endorsement of the thesis that systems of support need to be organised in such a way as to maximise the opportunities for teachers to engage in the kinds of reflective analysis of classroom experience proposed in this book. Indeed, it suggests a way of reconceptualising the notion of support as something additional to what is generally available for all that would, after all, be congruent with an inclusive approach.

Additional time for careful thinking

What would be additional would be the *extra attention* given to individual children, in the form of extra *thought* paid to their responses to classroom learning activities, beyond what it is possible (and necessary) for individual teachers *already* to be doing without additional support. But the support strategies which result would not necessarily lead to any identifiably extra or different *provision* being made for a particular child, because wherever possible (and appropriate) these would be incorporated into the ongoing experiences planned for the whole group.

Such an interpretation of 'support' could certainly lend itself to the construction of an IEP, if such a document as this was indeed felt to provide a useful tool for reflection, planning and review, as well as for recording what was currently being done to facilitate the learning of an individual child. (For an analysis and critique of IEPs, as currently being developed under the aegis of the *Code of Practice*, see Tod *et al.* 1998, Cornwall and Tod 1998 and Tod 1999.) Recorded in the plan would be current thinking about what might make a difference to the child's learning (based on the interpretation of information so far available), what action this implies at classroom or whole-school level, and what developments in the child's learning might be expected as a consequence. Targets could be formulated on the basis of these plans, if these were felt to assist in focusing thinking, although the Enfield group became increasingly convinced that the most effective targets were likely to be those that teachers set *themselves*, on the basis of their analysis. Their experience suggests, too, that it is important to keep things flexible and open-ended. The reflective analysis of classroom experience helps to clarify a general direction for the development of practice, but the ideas also need to evolve over time as teachers experiment with different ways of achieving the goals they have set themselves.

Innovative thinking and inclusion

The Enfield research thus helped to highlight a subtle, yet critically important, dimension to the task of fostering the progress and inclusion of children experiencing difficulties, bound up with interpersonal relationships and the reciprocal communication of acknowledgement. This implies it is not just the scope and substance of what we do that is important, but how we *think* about what we do, and the subtle messages that this thinking conveys to the learners who are the subject of our attention. The extent to which such an approach (based on giving *extra thought* to individuals) would succeed in safeguarding children's interests and increasing their participation and learning, would be ultimately dependent upon the nature and qualities of the thinking used to understand perceived difficulties and generate ideas for enhanced learning. It would depend upon the adequacy of the analysis carried out, the kinds of questions that were asked and the range of possibilities that were considered for further supporting the child's learning.

In presenting the framework for innovative thinking, I have argued that an adequate understanding of children's classroom responses requires an analysis that remains focused on the detail of children's engagement with classroom learning experiences and that, as a minimum, takes account of all the features of the situation reflected in the five questioning moves:

- the relationship between children's responses in the immediate situation and features of the classroom context, overall school context, and the wider context of children's learning in home and community;
- how the teacher's particular resources, beliefs and values shape the meanings constructed from the evidence;
- children's own meanings, purposes, feelings, agendas;
- how the teacher's feelings affect the meanings bestowed on the situation;
- how the inescapable limitations of the knowledge and information which the teacher currently has available affect these meanings.

In this chapter, I have argued that the same approach to analysis needs to lie at the heart of schools' systems of support for children perceived to be experiencing difficulties. This will help to ensure that, while the analysis remains squarely focused on the distinctive qualities and characteristics of individual responses, concerns *about* individuals are not treated as problems *of* individuals; and that every effort is made to explore ways of interpreting children's classroom responses other than as a reflection of personal characteristics and limitations.

Moreover, the same qualities of thinking that, I have argued, enable teachers to fulfil their responsibilities towards children generally *also* have a critical part to play in the development of schools' capacity for inclusion. As Ainscow notes:

Progress towards the creation of schools that can foster the learning of all children will only occur where teachers become reflective and critical practitioners capable of and empowered to investigate aspects of their practice with a view to making improvements. Only in this way can we overcome the limitations and dangers of deficit thinking; only in this way can we be sure that pupils who experience difficulties in learning can be treated with respect and viewed as potentially active and capable learners.   (Ainscow 1998: 11–12)

Innovative thinking is also *inclusive* thinking. The careful, ongoing, reflective analysis of classroom events and the routine questioning of interpretations affords an ever-present opportunity for negative identities to be renegotiated, and for genuine acknowledgement to evolve; it also ensures that careful consideration is continually given to whatever might be done, beyond what is currently being done, to overcome barriers and enhance children's participation and learning *within* mainstream classrooms.

The task of working towards a more inclusive education system necessarily involves intervention at a number of different levels, some beyond the control of individual schools. However, it is important to emphasise that what teachers do every day in their classrooms – and afterwards when they reflect on their work – is also of critical importance. As Emer's experience with Costas illustrates, even the most fleeting encounters with children play a part in the dynamics of inclusion and exclusion. The thinking that we do during and after teaching determines whether or not new perspectives on classroom events are opened up; whether or not experience provides a continual, self-replenishing source of ideas to guide the development of practice.

When teachers have time, and perceive a need, to process classroom experience in such a way as to open up new possibilities, their thinking becomes an essential creative force which drives the process of inclusion. Innovative thinking is both a vital source of new ideas in its own right, and an essential means by which ideas derived from external sources are successfully incorporated into existing ways of working in order to aid children's learning and their inclusion in the work of the whole class. Indeed, it is important not to overlook the important part that general developments in practice can play in enhancing the participation and learning of children experiencing difficulties. Although the *Code of Practice* nowhere acknowledges this, it is not always necessary to start from a focus on particular individuals in order to generate ideas for enhancing teaching and learning that directly benefit individual children. There are many promising ideas arising from current literature and research which, if introduced into general curriculum practices, might be of especial help to those experiencing difficulties while also benefiting *all* pupils. For example, the enhancement of formative assessment (as proposed by Black and Wiliam 1998); approaches to differentiation (e.g. McNamara and Moreton 1998); strategies for enhancing subject learning and literacy learning across the curriculum (e.g. Wray and Lewis 1997; Counsell 1997; Webster *et al.* 1996); and strategies for enhancing thinking skills (e.g. Adey and Shayer 1994; McGuinness 1999).

However, while ideas from external sources (from other colleagues, from the literature, from research) can suggest promising directions for development and often useful practical guidance, they cannot foresee the very specific questions and challenges that arise when suggested approaches are tried out with a new group of learners, in a new setting, and by a teacher for whom this is a relatively unfamiliar way of working. The success of any new strategy intended to enhance learning and inclusion depends ultimately upon practitioners' thinking: their ability to interpret the feedback provided by children, and sensitively adjust and refine practices in the light of children's responses.

This is why it is so important, if there is a genuine commitment to developing a more inclusive education system, to maximise mainstream teachers' opportunities to reflect upon their experience in the ways proposed in this book. The accounts in Chapters 8 and 9 show that the task of 'providing effective learning opportunities for all pupils' (DfEE/QCA 1999) is a developmental one which depends not just upon careful planning but also upon teachers' ability to process classroom experience in a way that opens up new possibilities. The organisation of support for children experiencing difficulties is one area of school work where opportunities naturally arise for teachers to work collaboratively to review and develop their thinking and practice, and use a specific focus on the needs of individuals as a stimulus for encouraging learning and achievement for all.

CHAPTER 12

Theories of teachers' thinking

The most important test for the ideas in this book, from my point of view, is that practitioners who encounter them experience a moment of recognition, and then find themselves empowered to use the ideas in a variety of ways to assist their own thinking. Since the ideas were originally derived from my own experience, it was only by sharing the framework with other teachers and finding out how they responded to it that I could discover if, as I anticipated, the five questioning moves were recognised as ways of thinking already used by teachers, and if making them explicit was experienced by teachers as helpful. So far, teachers who have encountered the ideas do usually seem to experience that moment of recognition. This book is also testimony to the practical utility of the framework, as reported by some of the practitioners who have used it to support their own thinking and professional development.

However, it is perhaps important, too, in conclusion, to consider where these ideas stand in relation to other views of teachers' thinking reflected in the literature. Readers familiar with research in this area will no doubt have observed that innovative thinking presupposes a view of teaching which is, in part, consciously reflective and analytical. It assumes that classroom teaching requires the development of sophisticated reflective and analytical skills, which are also available for teachers to deploy outside the classroom for the purposes of reviewing and reflecting on their work.

Yet such a view is in marked contrast to other prevalent accounts of teacher expertise which characterise expert thinking as essentially intuitive: the deployment of craft knowledge which is, for the most part, tacit and unarticulated. My view has closer affinities with theories of reflective practice and action research; yet there are also differences. It may be useful, therefore, in this final chapter, to take a fresh look at some of these different theories of teachers' thinking, and at the evidence that supports them, in order to articulate more fully the basis for the view of reflective teaching presented here.

The origins of my own view

In *Beyond Special Needs,* I explain in detail the processes which led me to identify the five questioning moves in the course of my own research (Hart 1994; 1996). I was not purposely studying teachers' thinking. Rather, I was grappling with a methodological dilemma of how to justify choosing between the many conflicting possible interpretations of children's responses that occurred to me, in a situation where I had the unaccustomed luxury of unrestricted time to think things through. As I thought about the consequences, for children, of eliminating – or perhaps not even considering – some of these interpretive possibilities, I became convinced that the task was not to establish a sound basis for *deciding between* interpretations; rather, it was to ensure that, in arriving at a particular interpretation, everything relevant to understanding the situation had been taken into account. The framework of questioning moves was constructed by noting patterns emerging among various interpretations of the same events, and by noting particular features of the situation that interpretations focused upon or left unexamined. I began to recognise the moves' potential as a vehicle for professional learning, when I realised that the process of checking out interpretations from these different perspectives was also *developmental*, enabling us to see new possibilities, and reach new understandings that could guide the development of practice.

In Chapter 2, I explored how the individual questioning moves relate to processes of interpretation that (according to my theory) teachers employ spontaneously in practice. I initially used my own experience to establish these links and so confirm, in a preliminary way, that the framework might be considered simply as a metacognitive tool, empowering teachers' thinking by virtue of naming and describing interpretive processes that teachers already use (at least to some extent) to make sense of what is happening in their classrooms.

While I was developing these ideas, and before I reached the point where I was ready to share them with other teachers, I drew on the work of Donald Schon (with some reservations (Hart 1995)) to provide support for the view of reflection that was emerging. Schon (1983) presents a view of professional thinking as involving sophisticated processes of reflection in the midst of action. Although he does not identify and name specific interpretive strategies, his account of reflective practice has many resonances with my account of innovative thinking:

> When a practitioner reflects in and on his practice . . . (he) may reflect on the tacit norms and appreciations which underlie a judgement, or on the strategies and theories implicit in a pattern of behaviour. He (sic) may reflect on the feeling for a situation in which he has framed the problem he is trying to solve, or on the role he has constructed for himself within the larger institutional framework.
>
> (Schon 1983: 62)

Schon distinguishes between 'knowing in action' and 'reflection in action'. Knowing-in-action refers to the ability of professional practitioners to respond spontaneously, intuitively and intelligently to the complex, ever-changing situations of practice, but without necessarily being aware, or able to offer an account, of how they arrive at the judgements implicit in their practice. Reflection-in-action is triggered when something unexpected, pleasing or puzzling, happens:

> When the phenomenon at hand eludes the ordinary categories of knowledge-in-practice, presenting itself as unique or unstable, the practitioner may surface and criticise his initial understanding of the phenomenon, construct a new description of it, and test the new description by on-the-spot experiment. (Schon 1983: 62–3)

Schon's account of professional thinking thus recognises the use of both intuitive, tacit expertise *and* highly sophisticated reflective, analytical expertise when circumstances allow and require a more inquiring approach. His work has been so widely taken up by teachers, teacher-educators and researchers that it would appear to be describing reflective activities with which experienced practitioners can readily identify.

Teaching as the intuitive deployment of craft knowledge

Yet Schon's account of reflection-in-action is by no means universally accepted in the field. Brown and McIntyre (1993), for example, suggest that the reason that Schon's account of teaching has been so enthusiastically espoused by many educationists is because it reflects their view of what teaching *ought* to be like, not what it actually *is* like. Certainly, the actual evidence that Schon provides in *The Reflective Practitioner* to support his view is scant, and is derived primarily from studies of professional practice other than teaching.

McIntyre (1998) puts forward a somewhat different view of teaching, based on a review of the literature and his personal research. He argues that the conditions of classroom life require teachers to develop forms of expertise that are automatic, intuitive and essentially non-reflective in nature. In order to achieve a competent and fluent performance in a complex situation characterised by multi-dimensionality, simultaneity, immediacy and unpredictability (Doyle 1986), they develop routines, which they deploy spontaneously, drawing on their craft knowledge, i.e.:

> the knowledge which teachers acquire primarily through their practical experience in the classroom, which guides their day to day activity in classrooms but is for the most part not articulated in words and which is brought to bear spontaneously, routinely and sometimes unconsciously on their teaching.
>
> (Brown and McIntyre 1993: 17)

Recognising that theories of teaching in the existing research literature were frequently not derived from the study of actual classroom practice, Brown and McIntyre carried out their own study, reported in *Making Sense of Teaching* (1993). Twelve secondary teachers and four primary teachers were observed teaching a complete unit of work, and after each lesson were invited to share their thoughts about 'those aspects of their teaching that had particularly pleased them, what they felt they had done well or what had given them satisfaction' (Brown and McIntyre 1993: 32).

Through the research, Brown and McIntyre developed a more elaborated view of teachers' spontaneous deployment of their craft knowledge through the use of various 'routines'. A routine was defined as a 'standardized pattern of action which a teacher undertakes recognising that certain conditions are impinging on his/her teaching, in order to maintain particular desired states of pupil activity or promote specific kinds of progress' (1993: 83). The researchers found that teachers were generally unable to explain the processes that led to the selection of particular routines, and this tended to confirm the view that teachers' interactive thinking was not consciously deliberative.

As Brown and McIntyre acknowledge, however, their findings might have been different had they asked teachers to focus on *problems* in their teaching, rather than what went well. It may be that, by focusing on what went well, teachers were drawn into a 'summative' style of thinking. If they had been asked to focus on concerns, and consider how they might attempt to change the situation for the better in future lessons, they might have been encouraged to display their expertise in more formative styles of analysis and theorising. In Schon's work and in other literature which focuses on the reflective expertise of professional work, it is always awareness of a problem, puzzle, or a mismatch between values and practice that shifts our thinking from its spontaneous, intuitive mode into its critical, reflective mode (e.g. Dewey 1932; Schon 1983; Elliott 1991; Brookfield 1995). A major review of research into teachers' thought processes (Clark and Peterson 1986: 275) also makes a similar point: 'As one teacher put it when he was asked if he was thinking of any alternative actions and strategies "At this point? No. None at all. It was going along. The only time I think of alternative strategies is when something startling happens"'.

Furthermore, if it is the case that the knowledge and expertise that distinguishes experienced from inexperienced teachers is largely tacit and embedded in their spontaneous, intuitive action, then it would seem unlikely that they would be easily able to bring that knowledge and expertise into play *outside* the context of actual teaching. Yet in a study of mathematics teaching (Desforges and Cockburn 1987), it was found that the teachers involved were able to make use of sophisticated reflective and analytic skills in their analysis of videos of their own and one another's teaching: 'The teachers . . . demonstrated the qualities of their own insight during the analysis of video tapes and in their comments on the mathematics schemes. Their capacity to spot problems, generate hypotheses and weigh alternative considerations *left little to be desired*' (Desforges and Cockburn 1987: 125, my emphasis).

But if, as McIntyre (1998) claims, the immediacy of teaching leads to the development of predominantly non-reflective, intuitive modes of expertise, how did the teachers *develop* the analytical and reflective skills which they displayed outside the classroom? Was it perhaps developed through experience of reflecting *on* their classroom experience, as a natural part of the planning-teaching-review cycle? Or was it, as Schon suggests, through reflecting upon questions arising in the midst of practice – and in spite of the many pressures which constrain opportunities to reflect?

In *Making Sense of Teaching*, no distinction is made between thinking immediately prior to decision-making and the *re-evaluation* of thinking immediately afterwards, in response to the feedback provided by pupils' responses to action previously taken. Yet in Schon's terms, reflection-in-action (like reflection-on-action) is, in part at least, a *retrospective* process which involves trying to *re*frame or *re*formulate existing thinking, when spontaneous, intuitive thinking has run into difficulties. It may be that it is the retrospective dimension of classroom thinking that researchers' questioning needs to focus upon if we are to advance insight into the use and development of teachers' reflective expertise.

Moreover, a view of professional expertise as heavily reliant on intuitive judgement is not necessarily incompatible with a view of professional expertise as also involving reflection. A close reading of the argument of Dreyfus and Dreyfus (1986) (to which Brown and McIntyre make approving reference in their critique of reflection-in-action), reveals a view of expert practice that does still include recognition of the need for a reflective capacity to operate alongside intuitive ways of thinking and knowing. While Dreyfus and Dreyfus argue that expert practice becomes more intuitive and less reflective as it evolves through various stages (analysis and reflection being characteristics of the thinking of novices not experts), they also acknowledge that intuitive judgement is not infallible; there must be potential for self-correction. To provide for this, they introduce into the analysis the notion of 'deliberative rationality': a process whereby experts operate self-critically upon intuitive judgement. When decisions are sufficiently important, or when time permits, practitioners stop using intuition and try to find other ways of seeing the situation. The process is described as follows:

> Aware that a current clear perception may well be the result of a chain of perspectives with one or more weak or questionable links, and so might harbour the dangers of tunnel vision, the wise intuitive manager will attempt to dislodge his current understanding. He will do so by rethinking the chain of events that led him to see things in the way that he does, and at each stage he will intentionally focus on elements not originally seen as important to see if there is an alternative intuitive interpretation.
> (Dreyfus and Dreyfus 1986: 165)

Indeed, right at the end of the analysis, they suddenly admit to the need for a small part of the mind – the 'monitoring mind' – *always* to remain aloof and detached in order to decide 'when results justify reinforcement of chosen actions or when events indicate that expectations or decisions should be modified' (Dreyfus and Dreyfus 1986: 40).

It seems, then, that there are a number of questions that might legitimately be raised about the evidence that supports a 'craft knowledge' view of teaching, and about the thesis that classroom conditions necessitate the development of forms of expertise that are essentially non-reflective. Most importantly, perhaps, we need to ask where this craft knowledge view of teaching stands in relation to the practice of all those teachers who, inspired by the work of Stenhouse (1975), Elliott (1991), McNiff (1993), Dadds (1995), Pollard (1996), Winter (1989) and many others, have committed themselves to enacting in their own work a view of teaching as a process of ongoing reflection, inquiry and action research.

Reflective teaching and action research

Although it would be misleading to imply that there is consensus among proponents of teaching as a reflective practice (Zeichner 1994), the view of teaching that supports innovative thinking has much closer affinities with this alternative tradition. Elliott (1991), for example, describes how teachers in his school in the 1960s became involved of their own accord in curriculum development as a response to the disaffection and alienation of the youngsters in their secondary modern school.

> Faced with both passive resistance and active rebellion, teachers in secondary moderns had two choices. The first was to develop and maintain a system of coercive control: to turn secondary moderns into concentration camps. The second was to make the curriculum more intrinsically interesting for the students and transform the examination system to reflect such change.   (Elliott 1991: 4)

The teachers drew on their collective knowledge and understanding to generate hypotheses about how to engage students more actively in curriculum tasks, implement their plans and then use the feedback provided by student responses to review, refine and adapt their original hypotheses in the light of their developing understandings. The new hypotheses would then become the occasion for the development of new plans.

> Curriculum practices were not derived from curriculum theories generated and tested independently of that practice. They constituted the means by which we generated and tested our own and each other's theories. Practices took on the status of hypotheses to be tested. So we collected empirical data about their effects and used it as evidence in which to ground our theorising with each other in a context of collegial accountability. We didn't call it research, let alone action-research ... But the concept of teaching as reflexive practice and a form of educational inquiry was tacitly and intuitively grasped in our experience of the innovation process.   (Elliott 1991: 8)

The ongoing questioning and development of practice which Elliott describes, driven by teachers' commitment to improve educational experiences for young people, has much in common with the approach presented in this book. Elliott is keen to emphasise that reflection and research are not additional activities for practitioners; they are integral features of teachers' pedagogical role:

> All too often research is viewed as something teachers now do *on* their practice. They step out of their pedagogical role. Teaching and research become posited as separate activities, whereas from the standpoint of the practitioner reflection and action are simply two aspects of a single process.   (Elliott 1991: 14)

However, there are also differences between Elliott's view of reflective practice and the view of teaching that supports innovative thinking. My view, like Schon's, assumes that teaching expertise includes *both* a spontaneous-intuitive dimension *and* a critical-reflective dimension, the latter being a mode of thinking that we move into when something occurs which puzzles, surprises or worries us, or which presents a problem for practice because it does not seem to fit our expectations or respond to our usual solutions. Elliott, on the other hand, sees 'action research' as a new form of professionalism, destined to *replace* 'non-reflective, intuitive and highly routinized' forms of practice (Elliott 1991: 55).

Moreover, although Elliott is keen to emphasise reflection as an integral feature of teachers' pedagogical practice, many practitioner accounts in the action research literature do seem to represent situations where teachers were indeed stepping *outside* their pedagogical role and doing research *on* their practice. These accounts provide evidence of the importance practitioners accord to reflection as part of a broad range of professional activities that might come under the heading of reflective practice; but they do not provide insight into, or directly support claims made for, reflection as an integral part of classroom teaching. Nor is strong empirical support for this view of teaching forthcoming from the literature on reflection. One survey, for example, of nine studies of professional reflection (Hayon 1990) revealed only one account (Schon's) which depicted reflection as taking place in the ongoing present; in all the other accounts, the time perspective for reflection was one of *retrospection*.

Teaching as interpretation and learning

Nevertheless, there *are* accounts of teaching, written by teachers themselves, where the practices described include reflection as an essential and integral part of the interactive processes of teaching. In these accounts, the act of teaching – the actual engagement of the teacher's mind with children's learning as it is happening – is presented in a way which clearly implies a conscious, sophisticated interpretive effort on the part of teachers. Reflection is clearly associated with classroom teaching, not with research (however defined) or with professional development activities which might be considered to be additional to the ordinary processes of teaching.

For example, teachers who espouse constructivist theories of learning inevitably commit themselves, if their practice is genuinely to reflect their espoused theories, to a reflective or inquiry approach to teaching. The teacher has to be continually seeking to penetrate the meanings which the child is constructing, and engaging with those meanings rather than simply imposing their own understanding on the child. In Chapter 5, for instance, we looked at the example of a secondary science teacher (Henderson 1996) attempting to understand and respond to a question by a student, Diane, during a lesson on gravitational pull. The teacher recalled what went through his mind as he attempted to make sense of her question and her difficulty. He illustrates the process of attempting to reconstruct his own thinking about the concept of gravitational pull, in the midst of teaching the whole class, by penetrating the different perspective of the student.

Further evidence is provided by the work of Paley (e.g. 1979; 1981; 1997a). Her open-ended, inquiring approach to teaching is illustrated in a fascinating series of books in which she explores the learning occasioned, year by year, and on a variety of different themes, by her work with children. In the last book written before she retired (1997a), she describes how the work of one author, Leo Leonni, came to dominate the school experience and learning of a particular group of children, another colleague and herself over the course of one school year. In the narratives she weaves around the group's individual and collective encounters with Leonni's stories, we see how events led her to question her own understandings and presuppositions, and how she allowed her thinking to be challenged and changed by the children's comments, perceptions and behaviour. Her reflections always end with a question because, in her approach, there is no final point of closure, only new insight which provides a springboard for further inquiry and learning. In a preface to a book on teachers' reflection, she describes the rationale underlying her approach as follows:

> Schoolteachers cannot escape this continual rethinking of interpretations and postulations; our students will not sit still long enough for definitive portraits and our wishes often supersede the actual event. Never can we say, 'There, it's done. I've explained it all'.
> (Paley 1997b: viii)

Other teachers whose values led them to espouse informal styles of education also describe their teaching as necessarily involving close observation and reflective inquiry:

> The teacher works at getting a clear and precise knowledge of the . . . cognitive growth of each child. To this end, she is constantly looking, listening, discussing and interpreting, bringing her intelligence and whole knowledge of children's learning to help guide her observations . . . A teacher must bring knowledge to bear on these observations, because the purpose is to be able to join the child in his efforts to learn and to do this in a way that is effective.
> (McKenzie and Kernig 1975: 44)

The active, interpretive role of the teacher is also emphasised by Michael Armstrong, whose approach to understanding children's writing was discussed in Chapter 4. It is further explored by Stephen Rowland (1987) who contrasts an interpretive approach to teaching with didactic and exploratory approaches. He argues that the attempt on the part of the teacher to understand the learner's present state of knowledge is an essential element of teaching. To achieve it requires negotiation between teacher and learners, with the teacher constantly asking himself 'Do I understand what the children are getting at?' His account of the teacher's task is echoed by James Britton, who refers to the interactive nature of teaching as 'a quiet form of research' (quoted in Miller 1987).

Practitioners whose values have led them to choose a mode of working which requires a sophisticated interpretive effort on the part of the teacher will no doubt *also* have developed forms of expertise that can also operate automatically, spontaneously, intuitively in order to create the space, within the constraints and pressures of working with large classes, to teach in a reflective and inquiring mode. We might surmise, therefore, that if any of these teachers had been among the participants in Brown and McIntyre's study, their accounts of their own expertise and 'success' in their teaching would have at the very least given grounds to question the generalisability of a view of teaching as an essentially non-reflective activity.

Developing dialogue about the place of reflection in teaching

What I conclude from this examination of different trends in the literature on teachers' thinking is that there is no single, secure knowledge base about the nature of teaching and teaching expertise in terms of which the legitimacy of new contributions can be judged. As a theory of how learning occurs through reflection, innovative thinking seeks to make a contribution to research in this area. There is clearly considerable scope for more research, although as Brown and McIntyre (1993) note, the methodological challenges are considerable. Perhaps, rather than starting out from the assumption that teachers don't have time to think, we need to be exploring what kinds of reflection teachers *do* spontaneously engage in and why, and how these are adapted to fit the circumstances of teaching. The starting assumption in this case would be that reflection in the context of teaching is likely to be something small-scale and localised, able to focus in on, inform and *transform* the minute detail of teachers' day-by-day judgements and interactions with children.

The teachers in the Enfield group provided many examples of such spontaneous reflection happening during the course of lessons as well as in their more conscious and deliberate reflection on their teaching after the event. In this book, I have emphasised the use of the framework mainly for retrospective thinking about teaching, because I am all too aware that the pressures of teaching large classes do not allow much time for considered thought in the midst of action. Yet it is also an important part of my argument that the moves are understood to be derived from interpretive strategies that teachers already use, moment-by-moment, to make sense of what is happening in their classrooms. If they are, then teachers are more likely to find the framework genuinely empowering. Otherwise, the framework could become just a set of procedures which straitjacket teachers' thinking rather than as a resource to be used flexibly in support of practitioners' own thinking. The more closely the moves correspond to ways of thinking that practitioners already use spontaneously, the more likely it is, I believe, that they will be able to exploit it creatively for their own purposes.

So far, as noted earlier, experience suggests that practitioners do recognise the moves and have found themselves able to use them in a variety of ways. In the Enfield group, some people used the framework consciously and deliberately to support their developing analyses. Others found it more comfortable to allow their thinking to flow freely, and then to use the moves retrospectively to ensure that they had not overlooked important features of the situation. Moreover, as people became more familiar with the moves to support their own thinking, they found themselves consciously choosing to make use of them in the course of their everyday teaching. I have described, for example, how Emer and Deb – as a result of the experience with Costas – made a conscious decision to try to take the child's eye view as a more conscious and deliberate feature of their teaching. Lesley Higgs has written persuasively, in Chapter 9, about how she used innovative thinking in a variety of professional situations.

Set against this experience, the thesis that the constraints of classroom teaching lead to the development of predominantly non-reflective modes of expertise does seem to underestimate the agency of teachers themselves in resisting those pressures and in shaping what happens – and what they want to happen in their classrooms – in line with their personal values and aspirations. While the pressures of classroom teaching clearly do impose major constraints on what is possible, the extent to which teaching is reflective is *also* a function of teachers' values and aspirations for children's learning, and the extent to which classroom practices have been developed and adjusted to reflect these.

The work with the Enfield research group, and with other teachers and professionals with whom the ideas have been shared so far, provides strong grounds for suggesting that others too will find the framework useful. The framework is presented, then, not as a final or definitive attempt to map out the questions that teachers do, can and need to ask when making sense of classroom events and checking out their spontaneous interpretations. Rather, it is a resource that teachers are invited to use and develop in whatever way that they see fit to assist them in this vital aspect of their professional work.

Bibliography

Abercrombie, M. L. J. (1989) *The Anatomy of Judgement: An investigation into the processes of perception and reasoning*. London: Free Association Books.

Adey, P. and Shayer, M. (1994) *Really Raising Standards*. London: Routledge.

Ainscow, M. (1998) 'Would it Work in Theory? Arguments for Practitioner Research and Theorising in the Special Needs Field', in Clark, C., Dyson, A. and Millward, A. *Theorising Special Education*. London: Routledge.

Ainscow, M. (1999) *Understanding the Development of Inclusive Schools*. London: Falmer Press.

Ainscow, M., Hargreaves, D., Hopkins, D., Balshaw, M. and Black-Hawkins, K. (1994) *Mapping Change in Schools. The Cambridge Manual of Research Techniques*. Cambridge: University of Cambridge.

Armstrong, M. (1990) 'Another Way of Looking', *Forum* **33**(1), 12–16.

Athey, C. (1990) *Extending Thought in Young Children: A parent–teacher partnership*. London: Paul Chapman Publishers.

Ball, S. (1981) *Beachside Comprehensive: A case study of secondary schooling*. Cambridge: Cambridge University Press.

Ball, S. (1993) 'Education policy, power relations and teachers' work', *British Journal of Educational Studies* **41**(2), 106–21.

Berliner D. C. (1987) 'Ways of thinking about students and classrooms by more and less experienced teachers' in Calderhead, J. (ed.) *Exploring Teachers' Thinking*. London: Cassell.

Bettelheim, B. and Zelan, K. (1991) *On Learning to Read: The child's fascination with meaning*. London: Penguin.

Black, P. and Wiliam D. (1998) *Inside the Black Box – raising standards through the curriculum*. London: Kings College School of Education.

Boaler, J. (1997) 'Setting, Social Class and Survival of the Quickest', *British Educational Research Journal* **23**(5), 575–95.

Brookfield, S. (1995) *Becoming a Critically Reflective Teacher*. San Francisco: Jossey Bass Publishers.

Brown, S. and McIntyre, D. (1993) *Making Sense of Teaching*. Buckingham: Open University Press.

Bruner, J. (1985) 'Vygotsky: A historical and conceptual perspective', in Wertsch, J. V. (ed.) *Culture, Communication and Cognition: Vygotskyan perspectives*. Cambridge: Cambridge University Press.

Clark, C. M. and Peterson, P. L. (1986) 'Teachers' thought processes', in Wittrock, M. C. (ed.) *Handbook of Research on Teaching*, 3rd edn. New York: Macmillan.

Claxton, G. (1990) *Teaching to Learn*. London: Cassell.

Cline, T. and Frederikson, N. (eds) (1996) *Curriculum Related Assessment, Cummins and Bilingual Children*. Clevedon: Multilingual Matters.

Connolly, P. (1998) *Racism, Gender Identities and Young Children: Social relations in a multi-ethnic, inner city primary school*. London: Routledge.

Cordingley, P. (1998) 'Teaching as a Research Based Profession', *NUT Educational Review* **11**, 2.

Cordingley, P. (1999) *Constructing and Critiquing Reflective Practice*. Paper presented at the conference 'Making Research Make a Difference', Cambridge 1999.

Cornwall, J. and Tod, J. (1998) *Individual Education Plans: Emotional and behavioural difficulties*. London: David Fulton Publishers.

Counsell, C. (1997) *Analytical and Discursive Writing at Key Stage 3*. The Historical Association.

Cummins, J. (1996) *Negotiating Identities: Education for empowerment in a diverse society*. Ontario: California Association for Bilingual Education.

Cummins, J. and Swain, M. (1986) *Bilingualism in Education: Aspects of theory, research and practice*. London: Longman.

Dadds, M. (1995) *Passionate Enquiry and School Development: A story about teacher action research*. London: Falmer.

Davies, L. (1984) *Pupil Power: Deviance and gender in school*. Lewes: Falmer Press.

Department for Education (1994) *Code of Practice on the Identification and Assessment of Special Educational Needs*. London: Stationery Office.

Department for Education and Employment (1997a) *Excellence in Schools*. Paper presented to Parliament by the Secretary of State for Education and Employment.

Department for Education and Employment (1997b) *Excellence for all Children: Meeting Special Educational Needs*. Paper presented to Parliament by the Secretary of State for Education and Employment.

Department for Education and Employment (1998a) *The National Literacy Strategy: Framework for Teaching*. London: DfEE.

Department for Education and Employment (1998b) *Meeting Special Educational Needs: A Programme of Action*. London: DfEE.

Department for Education and Employment (1999a) *The National Numeracy Strategy: Framework for Teaching*. London: DfEE.

Department for Education and Employment (1999b) *The National Literacy Strategy. Key Stage 3 Literacy Conferences*. LEA file. London: DfEE.

Department for Education and Employment/Qualifications and Curriculum Authority (1999) *The National Curriculum for England*. London: DfEE/QCA.

Department of Education and Science (1989) *Discipline in Schools*. Report of the Committee of Enquiry chaired by Lord Elton. London: HMSO.

Desforges, C. and Cockburn, A. (1987) *Understanding the Mathematics Teacher: A study of practice in first schools*. Lewes: Falmer.

Desforges, C. and McNamara, D. (1979) 'Theory and practice: methodological procedures for the objectification of craft knowledge', *British Journal of Teacher Education* **51**(2), 145–52.

Dewey, J. (1932) *How We Think: A restatement of the relation of reflective thinking to the educative process*. Boston: D. C. Heath & Co.

Donaldson, M. (1978) *Children's Minds*. London: Fontana.

Doyle, W. (1986) 'Classroom organisation and management', in Wittrock, M. C. (ed.) *Handbook of Research on Teaching*, 3rd edn. New York: Macmillan.

Dreyfus, H. L. and Dreyfus, S. E. (1986) *Mind Over Machine*. New York: Free Press.

Drummond, M. J. (1993) *Assessing Children's Learning*. London: David Fulton Publishers.

Drummond, M. J. (1995) 'The concept of competence in primary teaching', in McKenzie, P., Mitchell, P. and Oliver, P. (eds) *Competence & Accountability in Education*. Aldershot: Arena.

Drummond, M. J., Rouse, D. and Pugh, G. (1992) *Making Assessment Work: Values and principles in assessing young children's learning*. London: National Children's Bureau.

Easen, P. (1987) 'All at sixes and sevens', in Booth, T., Potts, P. and Swann, W. *Preventing Difficulties in Learning*. Oxford: Blackwell.

Easen, P. (1995) *Collaborative Learning and Children's Thinking*. Keynote lecture, annual conference of the Collaborative Learning Network, July 1995.

Easen, P., Kendall, K. and Shaw, J. (1992) 'Parents and educators: dialogue and development through partnership', *Children and Society* **6**(4), 282–96.

Elliott J. (1991) *Action Research for Educational Change*. Buckingham: Open University Press.

Frederikson, N. and Cline, T. (1996) 'A model of curriculum related assessment', in Cline T. and Frederikson, N. (eds) *Curriculum Related Assessment, Cummins and Bilingual Children*. Clevedon: Multilingual Matters.

Fullan, M. (1982) *The Meaning of Educational Change*. Ontario: Ontario Institute for Studies in Education.

Fullan, M. (1991) *The New Meaning of Educational Change*. London: Cassell.

Gillborn, D. (1990) *Race, Ethnicity and Education: Teaching and learning in multi-ethnic schools*. London: Unwin Hyman.

Gillborn, D. (1995) *Racism and Antiracism in Real Schools*. Buckingham: Open University Press.

Goleman, D. (1996) *Emotional Intelligence: Why it can matter more than IQ*. London: Bloomsbury.

Greenhalgh, P. (1994) *Emotional Growth and Learning*. London: Routledge.

Gregory, E. (1993) 'Sweet and sour', *Language in Education* **27**(3), 53–9.

Gregory, E. (1994) 'Cultural assumptions and early years pedagogy: The effect of the home culture on minority children's interpretation of reading in school', *Language, Culture and Curriculum* **7**(2), 111–24.

Griffiths, M. and Davies, C. (1995) *In Fairness to Children*. London: David Fulton Publishers.

Hall, D. (1996) 'Identifying needs', *Language Matters*. London: Centre for Language in Primary Education.

Hall, N. and Robinson, A. (1994) *Keeping in Touch: Using interactive writing with young children*. London: Hodder and Stoughton.

Hallam, S. and Toutounji, I. (1998) *What do we Know about the Grouping of Pupils by Ability? A research review*. London: Institute of Education, University of London.

Hargreaves, D. (1967) *Social Relations in a Secondary School*. London: Routledge and Kegan Paul.

Hargreaves, D. (1972) *Interpersonal Relations and Education*. London: Routledge and Kegan Paul.

Hargreaves, D. (1998) *Creative Professionalism: The role of teachers in the knowledge society*. London: Demos.

Hart, S. (1989) 'Everest in plimsolls', in Mongon, D. and Hart, S. *Improving Classroom Behaviour: New directions for teachers and pupils*. London: Cassell.

Hart, S. (1994) *The Innovative Practitioner: Reconceptualising the special needs task*. Unpublished Ph.D. thesis. London: University of Greenwich.

Hart, S. (1995) 'Action in reflection', *Educational Action Research* **3**(2), 211–32.

Hart, S. (1996) *Beyond Special Needs: Enhancing children's learning through innovative thinking*. London: Paul Chapman Publishers.

Hart, S. and Scott, S. (1987) 'Attractions of the North Pole', in Booth, T., Potts, P. and Swann, W. *Preventing Difficulties in Learning: Curricula for all*. Oxford: Blackwell.

Hart, S. and Travers, P. (1999) 'Bilingual learners and the Code of Practice', *Multicultural Teaching* **17**(2), 37–42.

Hayden, C. (1997) *Children Excluded from Primary Schools: Debates, evidence, responses*. Buckingham: Open University Press.

Hayon, L. K. (1990) 'Reflection and professional knowledge: A conceptual framework', in Day, C. *et al. Insight into Teachers' Thinking and Practice*. Basingstoke: Falmer.

Heath, S. B. (1983) *Ways with Words: Language, life and work in communities and classrooms*. Cambridge: Cambridge University Press.

Henderson, J. G. (1996) *Reflective Teaching: The study of your constructivist practices*, 2nd edn. Englewood Cliffs, NJ: Merrill.

Holt, J. (1990) *How Children Fail*, revised edn. London: Penguin.

Huberman, M. (1992) 'Teacher development and instructional mastery', in Hargreaves, A. and Fullan, M. G. (eds) *Understanding Teacher Development*. London: Cassell.

Hull, R. (1985) *The Language Gap: Why classroom dialogue fails*. London: Methuen.

Jackson, B. (1964) *Streaming: An education system in miniature*. London: Routledge and Kegan Paul.

James, M. and Worrall, N. (2000) 'Building a reflective community: development through collaboration between an HEI and one school over ten years', *Educational Action Research* **8**.

Keddie, N. (1971) 'Classroom knowledge', in Young, M. F. D. (ed.) *Knowledge and Control: New directions for the sociology of education*. London: Collier Macmillan.

Kelly, G. A. (1955) *The Psychology of Personal Constructs*. New York: Norton.

Kiddle, C. (1999) *Traveller Children: A voice for themselves*. London: Jessica Kingsley Publishers.

Lacey, C. (1970) *Hightown Grammar: The school as a social system*. Manchester: Manchester University Press.

Language and Curriculum Access Service (1995) *Making Progress. Teaching and assessment in multilingual classrooms*. London Borough of Enfield.

Language and Curriculum Access Service (1999) *Enabling Progress in Multilingual Classrooms: Towards inclusive education*. London Borough of Enfield.

Lewis, A., Neill, S. and Campbell, R. (1996) *The Impact of the Code of Practice in Primary and Secondary Schools: a national survey of the perceptions of special educational needs coordinators*. London: National Union of Teachers.

Lincoln, P. (1999) *Creating local frameworks to develop good practice and build professional knowledge: the role of the LEA*. Paper presented at the conference 'Making Research Make a Difference', University of Cambridge, School of Education, April 1999.

Mac An Ghaill, M. (1988) *Young, Gifted and Black: Student–teacher relations in the schooling of black youth*. Milton Keynes: Open University Press.

Mac An Ghaill, M. (1994) *The Making of Men: Masculinities, sexualities and schooling*. Buckingham: Open University Press.

Maybin, J., Mercer, N. and Stierer, B. (1992) '"Scaffolding" learning in the classroom', in Norman, K. (ed.) *Thinking Voices*. London: Hodder and Stoughton.

McGuinness, C. (1999) *From Thinking Skills to Thinking Classrooms: a review and evaluation of approaches for developing pupils' thinking*. London: Stationery Office.

McIntyre, D. (1998) *Has Classroom Teaching Served Its Day?* Paper presented at a research seminar held at University of Cambridge School of Education, November 1998.

McKenzie, M. and Kernig, W. (1975) *The Challenge of Informal Education: Extending young children's learning in the open classroom*. London: Darton, Longman and Todd.

McManus, M. (1987) *Troublesome Behaviour in the Classroom*. London: Routledge.

McNamara, S. and Moreton, G. (1998) *Understanding Differentiation: A teacher's guide*. London: David Fulton Publishers.

McNiff, J, (1993) *Teaching as Learning: An action research approach*. London: Routledge.

Miller, J. (1987) 'Teachers' emerging text: The empowering potential of writing in in-service', in Smyth, J. (ed.) *Educating Teachers: Changing the nature of pedagogical knowledge*. Lewes: Falmer.

Mirza, H. (1992) *Young, Female and Black*. London: Routledge.

Molnar, A. and Lindquist, B. (1989) *Changing Problem Behaviour in Schools*. San Francisco: Jossey Bass Inc., Publishers.

Mosley, J. (1996) *Quality Circle Time in the Primary Classroom: Your essential guide to enhancing self-esteem, self-discipline, and positive relationhips*. Wisbech: Learning Development Aids.

Nutbrown, C. (1999) *Threads of Thinking: Young children learning and the role of early education*, 2nd edn. London: Paul Chapman Publishers.

Paley, V. G. (1979) *White Teacher*. Cambridge, Mass.: Harvard University Press.

Paley, V. G. (1981) *Wally's Stories*. Cambridge, Mass.: Harvard University Press.

Paley, V. G. (1997a) *The Girl With the Brown Crayon*. Cambridge: Harvard University Press.

Paley V. G. (1997b) Foreword in Hall, A., Campbell, C. H. and Miech, E. J. *Class Acts: Teachers reflect on their own classroom practice*. Cambridge, Mass.: Harvard Educational Review reprint.

Parlett, M. (1991) 'The assessment of hearing impaired children', in Schon, D. A. (ed.) *The Reflective Turn: Case studies in and on educational practice*. New York: Teachers College Press.

Perera, K. (1979) 'The language demands of school learning', in the Open University, PE232 Language Development, *Supplementary Readings for Block 6*. Milton Keynes: Open University.

Perera, K. (1984) *Children's Writing and Reading: Analysing classroom language*. Oxford: Blackwell.

Pollard, A. (1985) *The Social World of the Primary School*. London: Cassell.

Pollard, A. (1996) *Reflective Teaching in the Primary School*, 3rd edn. London: Cassell.

Pye, J. (1988) *Invisible Children: Who are the real losers at school?* Oxford: Oxford University Press.

Rowland, S. (1987) 'Child in control: Towards an interpretive model of teaching and learning', in Pollard, A. (ed.) *Children and their Primary Schools*. Lewes: Falmer.

Salmon, P. (1995) *Psychology in the Classroom: Reconstructing teachers and learners*. London: Cassell.

Salzberger-Wittenberg, I., Henry, G. and Osborne, E. (1983) *The Emotional Experience of Learning and Teaching*. London: Routledge and Kegan Paul.

Sampson, C. (1994) 'Our journey of discovery', in Mason, M. and Rieser, R. *Altogether Better*. London: Comic Relief.

Schon, D. A. (1983) *The Reflective Practitioner: How professionals think in action*. New York: Basic Books.

Schon, D. A. (1988) 'Coaching reflective teaching', in Grimmett, P. P. and Erickson, G. L. (eds) *Reflection in Teacher Education*. New York: Teachers' College Press.

Searle, C. (1995) 'A different achievement: excellence in the inner city', *Forum* **38**(1), 17–20.

Seligman, M. (1991) *Learned Optimism*. New York: Knopf.

Stenhouse, L. (1975) *An Introduction to Curriculum Research and Development*. London: Heinemann.

Stirling, M. (1996) 'Government policy and disadvantaged children', in Blyth, E. and Milner, J. (eds) *Exclusion From School*. London: Routledge.

Swann, W. (1988) 'Differentiation or integration?', in Thomas, G. and Feiler, A. *Planning For Special Needs*. Oxford: Blackwell.

Tizard, B. and Hughes, M. (1984) *Young Children Learning: Talking and thinking at home and at school*. London: Fontana.

Tizard, B., Blatchford, P., Burke, J., Farquhar, C. and Plewis, I. (1988) *Young Children at School in the Inner City*. Hove: Lawrence Erlbaum Associates.

Tod, J. (1999) *Individual Education Plans: Dyslexia*. London: David Fulton Publishers.

Tod, J., Castle, F. and Blamires, M. (1998) *Individual Education Plans: Implementing effective practice*. London: David Fulton Publishers.

Watts, M. and Bentley, D. (1989) 'Constructivism in the classroom: enabling conceptual change by words and deeds', in Murphy, P. and Moon, B. (eds) *Developments in Learning and Assessment*. London: Hodder and Stoughton in association with the Open University.

Webster, A., Beveridge, M. and Reed, M. (1996) *Managing the Literacy Curriculum: How schools can become communities of readers and writers*. London: Routledge.

Wells, G. (1986) *The Meaning Makers: Children learning language and using language to learn*. London: Hodder and Stoughton.

White, R. and Gunstone, R. (1992) *Probing Understanding*. London: Falmer.

Willis, P. (1977) *Learning to Labour: How working class kids get working class jobs*. Farnborough: Saxon House.

Winter, R. (1989) *Learning from Experience: Principles and practice in action research*. Lewes: Falmer.

Winter, R. and Munn-Giddings, C. (forthcoming) *Doing Action Research: A theoretical and practical guide for health and social care*. London: Routledge.

Woods, P. (ed.) (1980) *Pupil Strategies: Explorations in the sociology of the school*. London: Croom Helm.

Wray, D. and Lewis, M. (1997) *Extending Literacy: Children reading and writing non-fiction*. London: Routledge.

Zeichner, K. (1994) 'Research on teacher thinking and different views of reflective practice in Teaching and Teacher Education', in Carlgren, I., Handal, G. and Vaage, S. (eds) *Teachers' Minds and Actions. Research on teachers' thinking and practice*. London: Falmer Press.

Index